SewFast
Gift Ideas
™

Quick Sewing Projects from Placemats

Quick Sewing Projects from Placemats

Susan Beck

Sterling Publishing Co., Inc.
New York

A Sterling/Sewing Information Resources Book

Owner: JoAnn Pugh-Gannon
Photography: Kaz Ayukawa, K Graphics
Illustrations: Susan Beck

Book Design and Electronic Page Layout: Ernie Shelton, Shelton Design Studios Inc.

Library of Congress Cataloging-in-Publication Data

Beck, Susan Parker.
    Quick sewing projects from placemats / Susan Beck.
        p.   cm. - - (SewFast gift ideas)
    "A Sterling/sewing information resources book."
    Includes index.
    ISBN 0-8069-9487-8
    1. Sewing.   2. Place mats.   3. Gifts.   I. Title.   II. Series.
TT705.B33 1996
746 - - dc20   96-26162
                                                                      CIP

A Sterling/Sewing Information Resources Book

2 4 6 8 10 9 7 5 3 1

Printed and distributed by Sterling Publishing Co., Inc.
387 Park Avenue South, New York, N. Y. 10016
Published and produced by Sewing Information Resources
P.O. Box 330, Wasco, Il. 60183
©1996 by Susan Beck
Distributed in Canada by Sterling Publishing
c/o Canadian Manda Group, One Atlantic Avenue, Suite 105
Toronto, Ontario, Canada, M6K 3E7
Distributed in Great Britian and Europe by Cassell PLC
Wellington House, 125 Strand, London WC2R 0BB, England
Distributed in Australia by Capricorn Link (Australia) Pty Ltd.
P.O. Box 6651, Baulkham Hills, Business Centre, NSW 2153, Australia
Printed in Hong Kong
All rights reserved

ISBN 0-8069-9487-8

DEDICATION

*To my mom, Norma, who
gave me many of the gift-giving
ideas seen in this book.*

SewFast
Gift Ideas

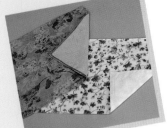

INTRODUCTION

No time to sew! With today's busy lifestyles, it's a problem most of us stitchers have. Our hectic schedules make it more and more difficult to find the time to make handmade gifts or even to stitch practical items for ourselves. This book offers a solution to this problem with more than 40 gift ideas that can be sewn quickly and easily—some in as little as 15 minutes!

The secret is that they all start with a purchased placemat—half of the work is done before you start. By taking advantage of the finished edges and the double sides, all it takes is a bit of clever folding and some easy stitching to turn these placemats into useful and fun everyday items. Don't be surprised if placemat shopping becomes as addictive as fabric shopping! The real fun is that once the project is made, no one will ever guess it started out as a placemat.

The success rate of making these items is almost 100%, even for the novice stitcher. In fact, most of these projects can provide an introductory experience for the new sewer. But even those of you who have been sewing for a few years are sure to find something appealing. Filled with gift ideas for the home, kids, travel, and office, this book offers an array of choices when gift-giving is in order. Try making the Hosiery Keeper and Padded Hanger in Chapter 2 as a shower gift. The Casserole Carrier in Chapter 3 is perfect for a housewarming or new neighbor gift —especially if it includes a tasty casserole with the recipe. The Mini Jewelry Case in Chapter 7 is quick to make and a perfect gift for the friend who travels. Many of the projects are practical ideas that are made for storing or organizing items around the house or in your sewing room. So when you are looking for ideas for gifts, keep in mind that it is nice to give yourself a gift once in awhile, too!

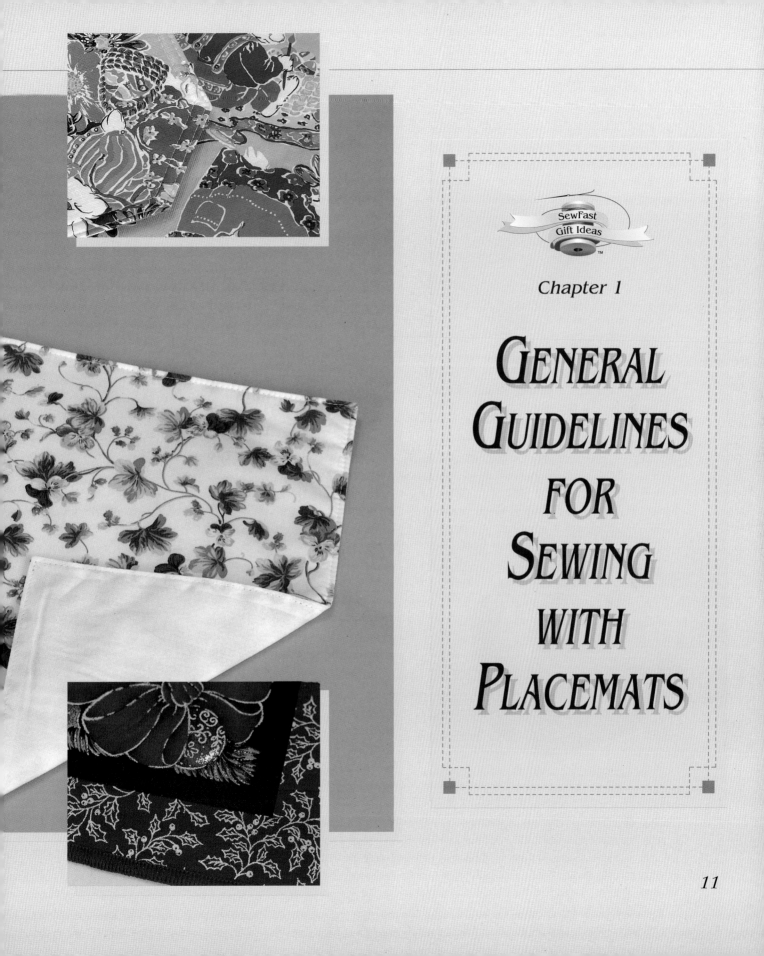

Chapter 1

GENERAL GUIDELINES FOR SEWING WITH PLACEMATS

*U*sing ready-made placemats instead of cut fabric offers several advantages to the home crafter and stitcher. One of the major pluses is that a project goes together much more quickly than when made from scratch. Placemats are usually double-sided so the project can be worked inside and out at the same time. Taking advantage of the finished edges of the placemats eliminates much of the finishing details of the item.

*P*lacemats, in a wide variety of fabrics and colors, are available at department stores, discount houses, and specialty linen shops. Shopping for placemats will become as much fun as shopping for fabric. When buying placemats to make any of the gift items in this book, be aware that the quality of workmanship varies a great deal. Similar styles and designs of placemats may be found both at upscale department stores and discount or outlet stores with a wide variance in price. Often the same manufacturer may produce a line for each type of retail store. The quality control may be different for the different retailers so don't always expect the same workmanship even when the placemats look similar. Irregulars or seconds will often work

well for these projects; however, there are some considerations to remember.

*I*f making an item that requires two or more placemats to be exactly the same size and shape, check this out when selecting them. There may be as much as 1/2" - 1" difference in placemats intended to be the same. For many projects, this will not be a problem, however, there may be cases where the sizing is more critical. Examine the edges of the placemats, as this is where there are often irregularities. Even the more expensive placemats should be looked over to see if they are suitable for the chosen project. The price does not always reflect the quality. The placemats used in this book cost from fifty cents on the clearance table to ten dollars at a high-end department store. Always check the sale table, especially if just one placemat is needed. Many times, the price of the placemat is reduced simply because there is only one left and most people are looking for two or more.

*C*are and cleaning of the sewn projects are usually simple matters because placemats are often made to withstand wear and washing. Most can be machine-washed and machine-dried, however there are some types that require dry cleaning. When using more than one type in a project, check the label and make sure that the methods of laundering are compatible. Placemats made of 100% cotton may shrink when washed for the first time, so it is best to prewash before stitching if the project is to be laundered after using.

There are several types of placemats available: unquilted cotton, quilted cotton, tapestry, woven cotton with and without fringed edges, vinyl, lace- or ruffle-edged, serged edges, and bound edges. All of these are readily available and work well for making various types of items. The directions in this book specify if a certain type is needed for a project, although in many cases, a variety of types will work equally well.

Placemats are found in a number of different shapes—rectangular, rectangular with rounded corners, oval, round, square, octagonal, and shaped (watermelon slice, country house, etc.). Most of these seem to be fairly easy to find in the retail stores that carry placemats. The round and square placemats are in the shortest supply, although with a bit of effort, they can be located.

Each project in this book begins with a list of materials that includes the type of placemat needed to make that particular item. The directions for many of the projects will include references to the right and wrong sides of the placemats. Since most placemats are double-sided, there really is not a right or wrong side. The choice is yours, and, in most cases, the references actually refer to the outside and inside of the item being made. Designating the right and wrong sides simply makes it a bit easier to explain the directions for making the item. So, make the decision before beginning the project and follow the directions accordingly.

After the listing of the type of placemat are measurements in parenthesis. These measurements tell the size of the placemat(s) used for the sample shown in the photograph. This is not intended to suggest that this is the only size that can be used to make the given project. A placemat that is somewhat smaller or slightly larger will probably give very satisfactory results. If a placemat of a different size is used, the measurements for folding, cutting, closure placement, and so on, may need to be adjusted to preserve the proportion of the item. One of the fun things about these projects is that there are no hard-and-fast rules of sewing perfection at work here. If a deeper fold or an extra line of stitching makes it work, then do what it takes. The key is to have fun and to end up with a useful item that you made yourself.

Most of the projects require very little cutting. The point is to cut as little as possible so there is less stitching required. When cutting is indicated, the finished edges of the placemat are utilized as much as possible, again to eliminate stitching and finishing work, therefore saving time and effort in producing these handmade creations. Cut edges can be finished in one of several different ways. The easiest is to turn under and stitch. Binding with bias tape or trimming with lace will also finish a cut edge. The project directions will instruct how it was done for the sample shown, but in most cases, the finishing method of your choice can be used.

Read the directions carefully and follow the illustrated steps for making these gifts. Spend an afternoon of sewing and you just might be able to take care of your gift list all at once!

MAKING PLACEMATS

You can make your own placemats instead of starting with purchased ones for great, quick gifts. All it takes is a yard of fabric for the front and a yard for the back to create 6 matching placemats. Add fleece or low-loft batting in the middle for a quilted effect. For a firm, crisp placemat, fuse interfacing to the wrong side of the front and/or back.

Materials:

Front - 1 yd of firmly woven fabric, 45" wide

Back - 1 yd of firmly woven fabric, 45" wide

fleece or low-loft batting (optional)

fusible interfacing (optional)

seam sealant (Serged version)

Directions:

CUTTING & PREPARATION:

Cut 6 fronts and 6 backs of the shape desired according to the layout below.

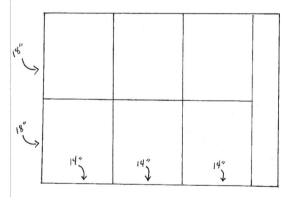

If a quilted or padded placemat is desired, cut batting the same size as the finished mat. Sandwich the batting between the front and back layers. Using a sewing machine, quilt the layers together in any pattern of stitching desired.

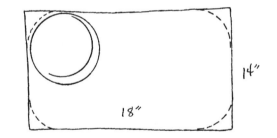

Use a saucer or small plate to round the corners.

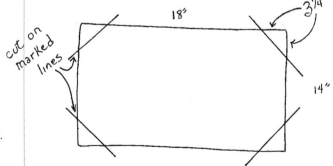

Make an octagonal shape, cutting the corners as marked. Finish each placemat using any of the following methods.

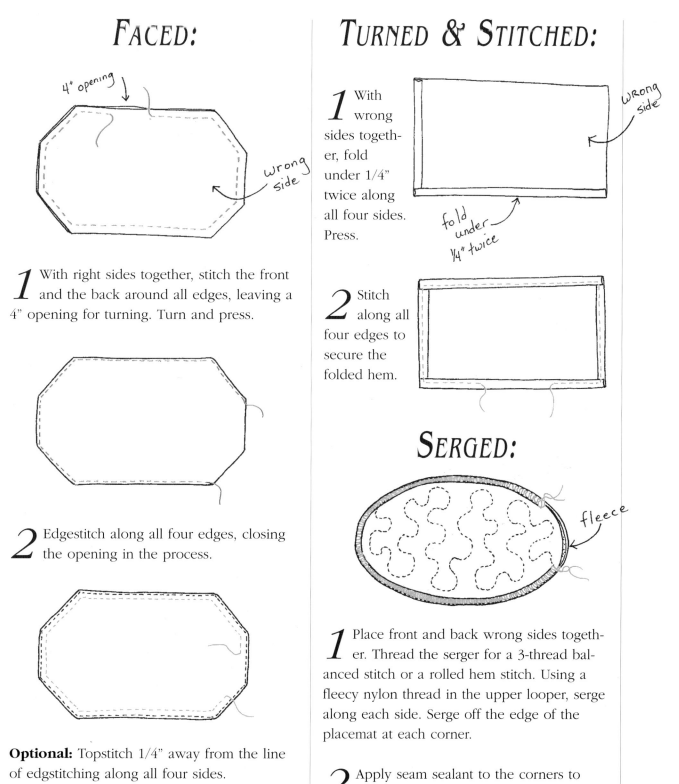

FACED:

1 With right sides together, stitch the front and the back around all edges, leaving a 4" opening for turning. Turn and press.

2 Edgestitch along all four edges, closing the opening in the process.

Optional: Topstitch 1/4" away from the line of edgstitching along all four sides.

TURNED & STITCHED:

1 With wrong sides together, fold under 1/4" twice along all four sides. Press.

2 Stitch along all four edges to secure the folded hem.

SERGED:

1 Place front and back wrong sides together. Thread the serger for a 3-thread balanced stitch or a rolled hem stitch. Using a fleecy nylon thread in the upper looper, serge along each side. Serge off the edge of the placemat at each corner.

2 Apply seam sealant to the corners to secure the threads. Clip the thread tails when the sealant is dry.

15

Chapter 2

THE
PERSONAL
TOUCH

*Keep your personal
items together in
the bedroom or
bath with these
simple placemat
projects.*

MAKEUP BRUSH ROLL-UP CASE

A compact way to keep makeup brushes together and ready to use. Great for travel!

Materials:

1 octagonal placemat(12" x 17")
1 yd of 1/2" satin ribbon
fabric marker

Directions:

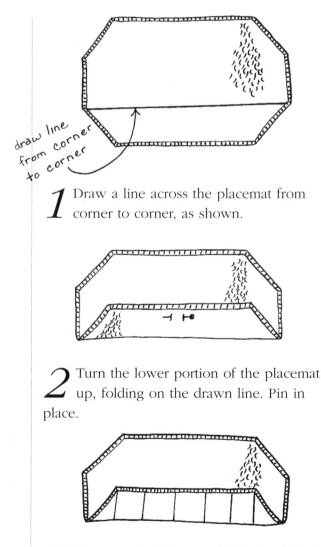

draw line from corner to corner

1 Draw a line across the placemat from corner to corner, as shown.

2 Turn the lower portion of the placemat up, folding on the drawn line. Pin in place.

3 Draw vertical lines to divide the folded flap into 5 (or more, if needed) sections.

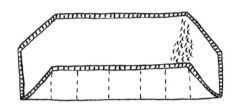

4 Using a decorative or a straight stitch, sew on the drawn lines to form pockets.

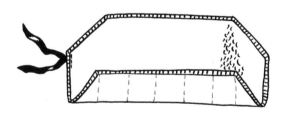

5 Fold the ribbon in half to find the center. Pin the center point of the ribbon to one edge of the placemat, positioning it near the upper corner. Bartack in place.

6 Place makeup brushes in the pockets. Roll up the case, starting at the end without the ribbon. Wrap the ribbon around the case and tie into a bow.

19

Easy Cosmetic Case

*A perfect companion to the Makeup Brush Roll-up Case,
make both of these in just a few minutes.*

Materials:

1 octagonal placemat(12" x 17")
4" of 5/8"-wide Velcro™

Directions:

Optional: To make the inside of the case spill-proof, laminate an iron-on vinyl to the wrong side of the placemat from corner to corner before beginning step 1.

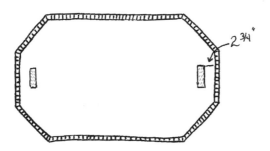

1 Stitch one Velcro™ half to the wrong side of the placemat at each end, centered from side to side and 2 3/4" from the edge.

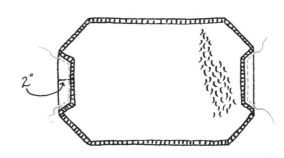

2 Fold back each end 2" to the right side and stitch along the edges to secure.

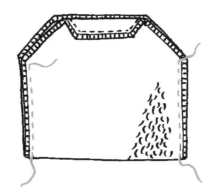

3 Fold in half with wrong sides together and the Velcro™ meeting. Stitch along the side edges to form a pocket.

HANGING JEWELRY ORGANIZER

Coordinate your jewelry with your favorite clothes by keeping them together in the closet!

Materials:

1 oval, ruffle or lace-trimmed placemat(17" x 14")
3 - 3"-square pieces of plastic canvas
1 yd of 1/4" ribbon
plastic hanger
10" of decorative cord
2 decorative buttons
1 large snap

Directions:

1 On the right side, mark a 4" line in the center of the placemat running across the width. Make a buttonhole using the marked line as a guide.

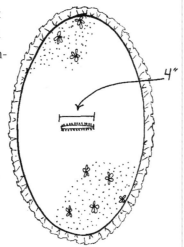

2 Bartack three 8" pieces of ribbon on the right side of the placemat 2" - 4" below the buttonhole. The ribbon placement can be staggered if desired. Tie the plastic canvas pieces onto the placemat using the ribbons.

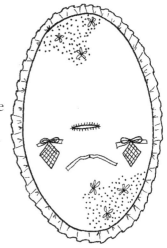

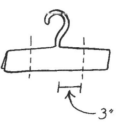

3 Position the cord across the placemat, under the plastic canvas pieces. Bartack across each end, at the hemline of the placemat, pulling the cord fairly tight with little slack to secure in place.

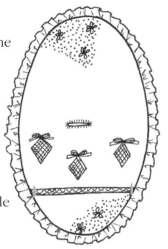

Optional: To make a holder for chains that don't have clasps, fold one end of the cord under and stitch to the hemline. Sew a snap on the under side of the other end of the cord and a corresponding snap on the placemat.

4 Sew a decorative button over each end of the cord.

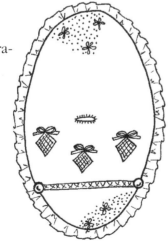

5 Cut or break the sides of the hanger to 3" in length on each side of the hook.

6 Slip the hook of the hanger through the buttonhole and fold the placemat in half. Stitch across the placemat under the hanger, using a zipper foot if necessary.

7 Attach earrings to the plastic canvas. Necklaces and chains hang on the cord and pins can be attached to the other side of the organizer.

HOSIERY KEEPER

Extend the life of delicate hosiery by keeping them in this pretty padded case.

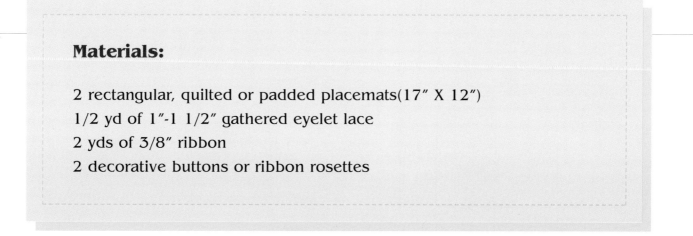

Materials:

2 rectangular, quilted or padded placemats(17" X 12")
1/2 yd of 1"-1 1/2" gathered eyelet lace
2 yds of 3/8" ribbon
2 decorative buttons or ribbon rosettes

Directions:

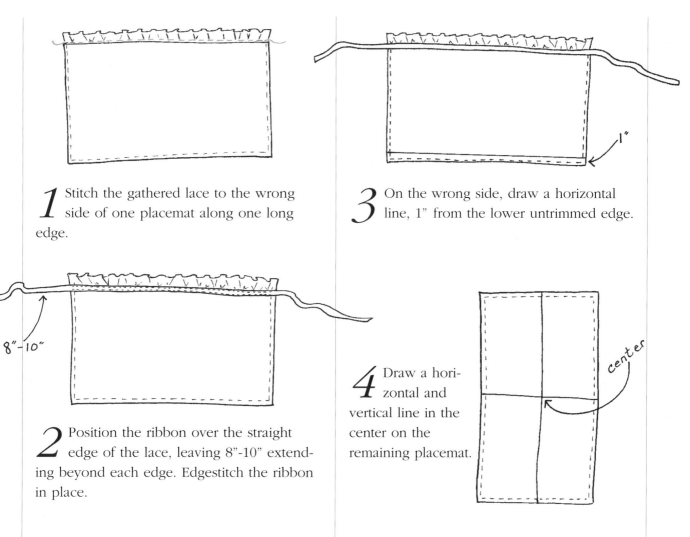

1 Stitch the gathered lace to the wrong side of one placemat along one long edge.

2 Position the ribbon over the straight edge of the lace, leaving 8"-10" extending beyond each edge. Edgestitch the ribbon in place.

3 On the wrong side, draw a horizontal line, 1" from the lower untrimmed edge.

4 Draw a horizontal and vertical line in the center on the remaining placemat.

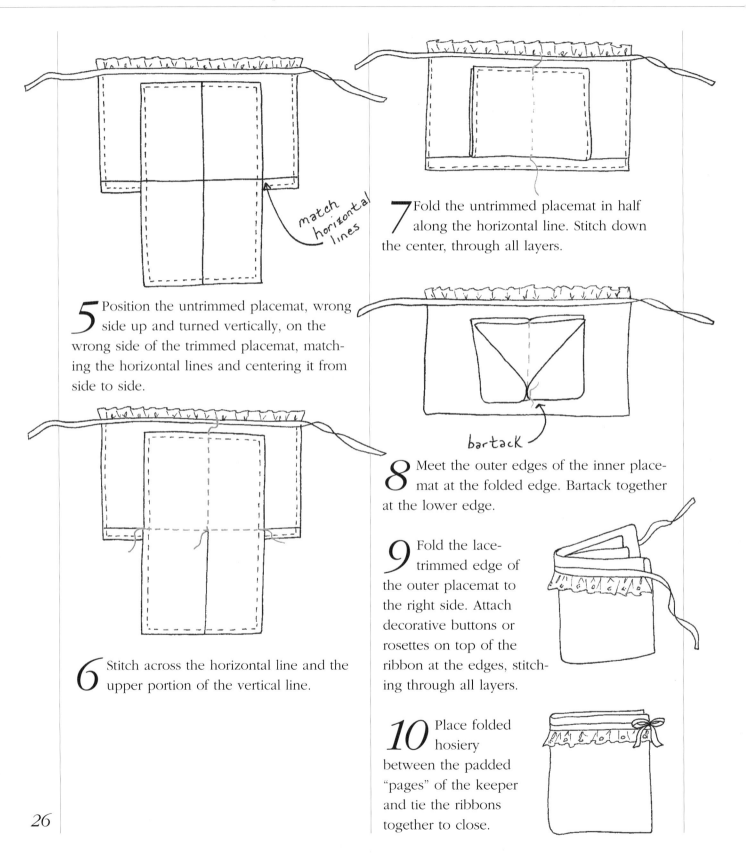

match horizontal lines

5 Position the untrimmed placemat, wrong side up and turned vertically, on the wrong side of the trimmed placemat, matching the horizontal lines and centering it from side to side.

6 Stitch across the horizontal line and the upper portion of the vertical line.

7 Fold the untrimmed placemat in half along the horizontal line. Stitch down the center, through all layers.

bartack

8 Meet the outer edges of the inner placemat at the folded edge. Bartack together at the lower edge.

9 Fold the lace-trimmed edge of the outer placemat to the right side. Attach decorative buttons or rosettes on top of the ribbon at the edges, stitching through all layers.

10 Place folded hosiery between the padded "pages" of the keeper and tie the ribbons together to close.

PADDED HANGER

Add this useful hanger to the Hosiery Keeper for a practical and pretty gift idea.

Materials:

1 rectangular, quilted or padded placemat(17" x 12")
1 wire or plastic-coated wire hanger (the placemat must be at
   least 1/4"-1/2" wider than the bottom edge of the hanger)
1 yd of 1"-1 1/2" gathered eyelet lace trim
1 yd of 3/8" ribbon
1 yd of 1/4" ribbon (optional)
2 small, shanked pearl buttons

Directions:

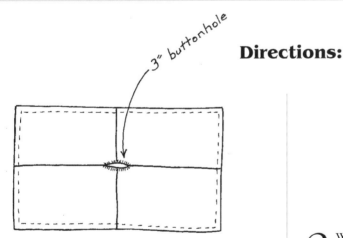

3" buttonhole

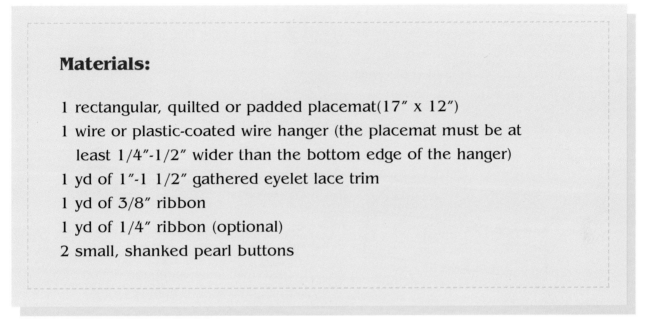

1 Draw a vertical and horizontal line in the middle of each edge on the placemat to find the center point. Make a 3" horizontal buttonhole at the intersection of these lines.

2 With wrong side out, fold the placemat in half across the width matching edges. Lay the hanger on the folded placemat with the hook extending past the folded edge at the buttonhole. Mark the slope of the sides of the hanger on the placemat.

27

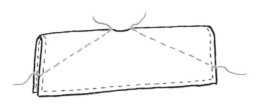

3 Using the marked lines as a guide, stitch two darts in the folded placemat, starting at the ends of the buttonhole.

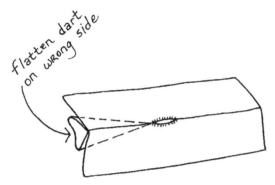

Flatten dart on wrong side

4 Turn the placemat to the right side and place over the hanger, putting the hook through the buttonhole. Flatten the darts so that each one folds over the hanger as padding.

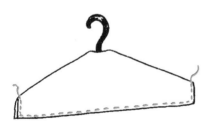

5 Using a zipper foot, stitch the sides and lower edges of the placemat together.

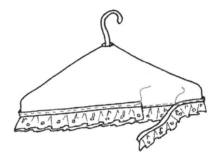

6 Stitch the ribbon along the straight edge of the eyelet lace trim.

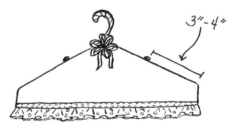

7 Beginning in the center of one side, pin the ribbon/lace to the lower edges of the placemat. Stitch along the ribbon edge, wrapping the trim to both sides.

3"–4"

8 If desired, wrap the hook of the hanger with 1/4" ribbon. Make a bow and hand-sew it to the cover at the hook. Hand-sew a button to each side of the hanger, 3" - 4" from each end. Use these buttons to keep narrow straps from slipping off the hanger.

BEDSIDE POCKET

This handy pocket can be stitched together in just five minutes. It provides a convenient place for eyeglasses, tissues, and nighttime reading material.

Materials:

1 rectangular, soft placemat of any type(18 1/2" x 13")

Directions:

1 With the placemat in a vertical position, fold the lower edge up 6" - 6 1/2" and pin in place.

2 Stitch along both side edges to secure the pocket.

3 Tuck the upper edge of the placemat between the mattress and the box springs of the bed and let the pocket hang below the mattress for use.

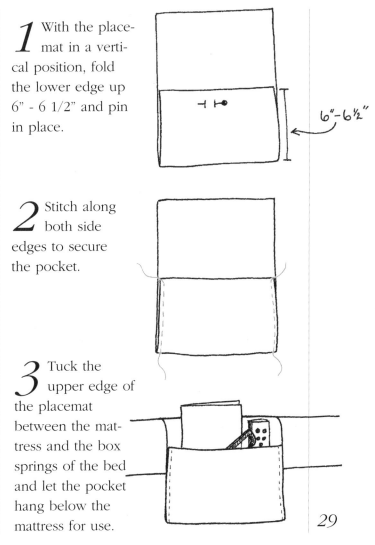

6"-6½"

29

ELEGANT DRESSER TRAY

*Keep perfume, jewelry, and trinkets in this
feminine accessory on your dresser.*

Materials:

1 rectangular, double-sided tapestry, damask, or similar fabric place-
  mat(18 1/2" x 13")
3 yds of 1 1/2"-wide wire-edged ribbon in a coordinating color
fabric marker

Directions:

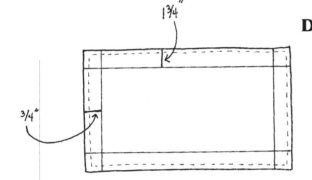

1 Draw a line 1 3/4" from each edge of the placemat.

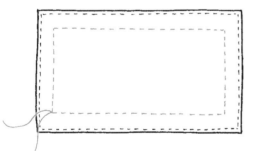

2 Using a straight-stitch, sew along the markings around the placemat using a coordinating color of thread.

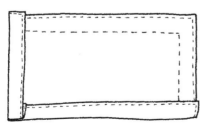

3 Fold the placemat edges in on the stitched lines and press.

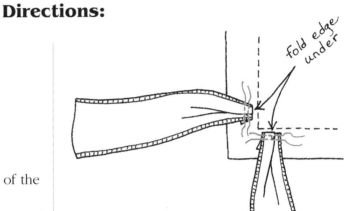

4 Cut the ribbon into eight equal pieces. Fold back 3/8" at one end of the ribbon pieces. Pleat the folded ends and place at the corners with the ribbons extending away from the place-mat. Stitch along the edge of the ribbons and again 1/8" away from the first stitching line.

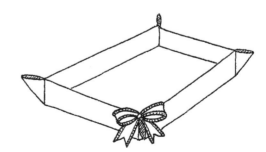

5 Tie the ribbons at each corner into a bow, forming the sides of the tray. Trim the ends of the ribbon in a "V" shape.

Chapter 3

AROUND
THE
HOUSE

*Accessorize your
home with these
handy, quick home
decorating projects.
And, they make
perfect housewarming
gifts, too!*

SIDE FLANGE PILLOW

*Create a warm, cozy feeling in any room
with this quick-to-make throw pillow.*

Materials:

2 rectangular, woven placemats(19" x 13")
1 - 10" or 12" square pillow form
fabric marker

Directions:

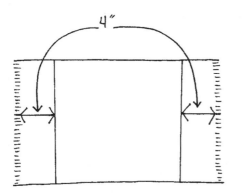

1 Using a fabric marker, draw vertical lines on the right side of one placemat, 4" from each end.

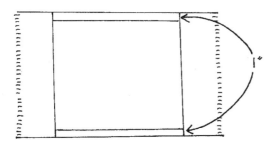

2 On the same placemat, draw horizontal lines 1" from each long edge between the marked vertical lines.

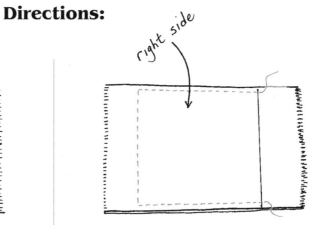

3 With wrong sides together, place the two placemats together with the marked one on top. Stitch, following the lines along one side, the top and the bottom, forming a pocket.

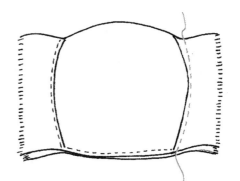

4 Insert the pillow form. Using a zipper foot, sew the remaining side closed following the drawn line.

35

NECK ROLL PILLOW

*A pleated placemat adds a tailored
look to this cylindrical pillow.*

Materials:

1 tuxedo placemat(18" x 12 1/2")
1 matching napkin(17" square)
1 yd of 3/8" ribbon in a matching or coordinating color
1 neck roll pillow form, 12" long x 15" in diameter

Directions:

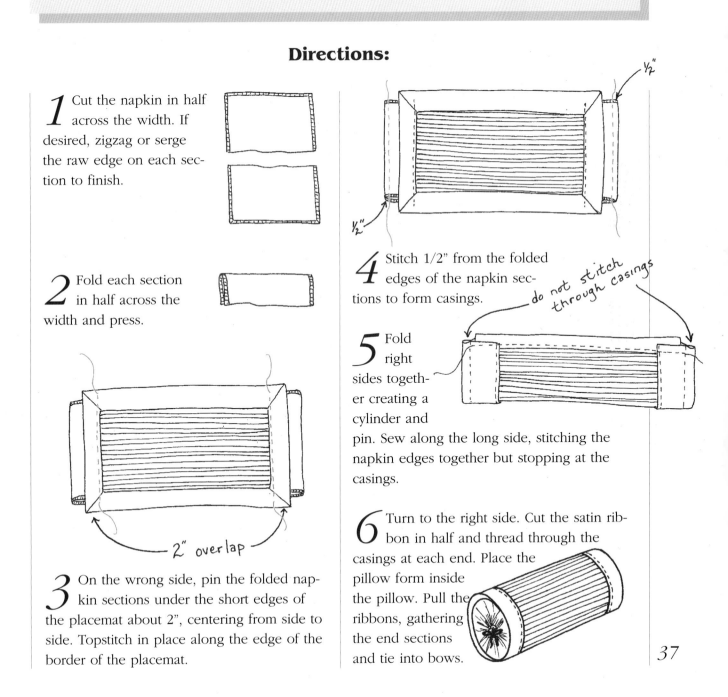

1 Cut the napkin in half across the width. If desired, zigzag or serge the raw edge on each section to finish.

2 Fold each section in half across the width and press.

3 On the wrong side, pin the folded napkin sections under the short edges of the placemat about 2", centering from side to side. Topstitch in place along the edge of the border of the placemat.

4 Stitch 1/2" from the folded edges of the napkin sections to form casings.

5 Fold right sides together creating a cylinder and pin. Sew along the long side, stitching the napkin edges together but stopping at the casings.

6 Turn to the right side. Cut the satin ribbon in half and thread through the casings at each end. Place the pillow form inside the pillow. Pull the ribbons, gathering the end sections and tie into bows.

2" overlap

do not stitch through casings

37

TEA COZY

Keep your tea warm by slipping this colorful
cozy over the teapot between pourings.

Materials:

2 oval, quilted or padded placemats(17" x 13")

6" of 1/2"-wide ribbon

1 yd of gathered eyelet lace (optional)

Directions:

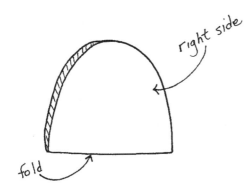

1 With the wrong sides together, fold each placemat in half across the short side.

2 Fold the ribbon into a loop and place the raw edges at the center of the upper edge of one placemat. Pin in place.

3 Pin the two folded placemats together with the ribbon loop to the outside and the raw edges between the two placemats. Stitch through all four layers around the curved edges along the hemline, securing the ribbon loop in the stitching.

CASSEROLE CARRIER

Keep foods warm while attractively transporting your casserole to parties and family get-togethers. This handy carrier will accommodate up to a 9" dish.

Materials:

2 octagonal, quilted placemats(16" x 13")
6" of 3/4"-wide Velcro™

Directions:

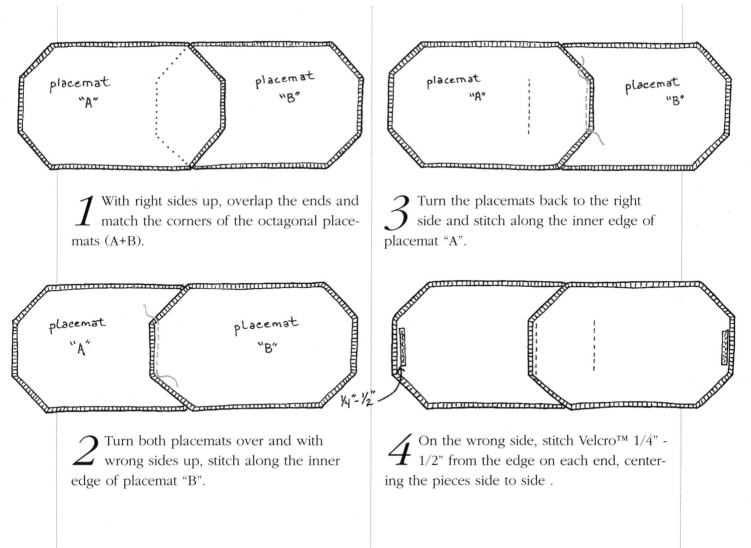

1 With right sides up, overlap the ends and match the corners of the octagonal placemats (A+B).

3 Turn the placemats back to the right side and stitch along the inner edge of placemat "A".

2 Turn both placemats over and with wrong sides up, stitch along the inner edge of placemat "B".

4 On the wrong side, stitch Velcro™ 1/4" - 1/2" from the edge on each end, centering the pieces side to side .

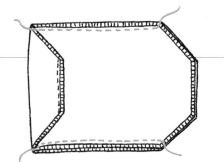

5 Fold the placemats, wrong sides together, matching the Velcro™ pieces. Using a narrow zigzag, stitch along the long sides only.

6 With the pocket on top, place a covered casserole dish into the carrier and press the Velcro™ together to close. Insert a spoon into the open pocket on the carrier.

MICROWAVE BREAD
WARMER

Use this easy pocket for bread and rolls for a quick warm-up in the microwave.

Materials:

1 octagonal placemat(18″ x 13″)
1/2 yd of 1/2″-wide grosgrain
ribbon

Directions:

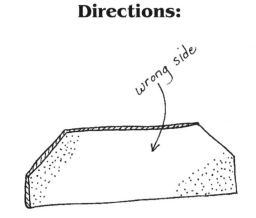

wrong side

1 With right sides together, fold the place-mat in half lengthwise.

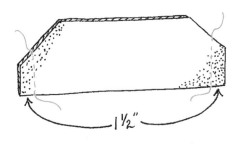

1½″

2 Stitch along each end, 1 1/2″ from the edges. Turn to the right side.

3 Cut the ribbon into two pieces. Turn under the raw edges of each ribbon piece and stitch one piece to the center of each side along the upper edges. To use, place bread or rolls in the pocket and loosely tie the ribbons together.

WINE BOTTLE COZY

Keep the chill on your next bottle of wine with this quick, quilted cover. It makes a great housewarming wrap for giving that special bottle of champagne.

Materials:

1 rectangular, double-sided, quilted placemat (17" x 13")
1 decorative button (optional)

Directions:

1 Roll the placemat into a cylinder, overlapping the edges 5". Stitch the overlapped sections together along the bottom edge. Do not sew the bottom of the cylinder closed.

— 5" overlap

2 Place a hand- or machine-stitched bartack through the overlapped section, 4" up from the bottom edge.

4"

3 On the opposite end, fold the upper and front edges of the cylinder back to form a collar and lapel. Bartack in place, close to the fold, if necessary, to help the cozy keep its shape. As an optional decoration, stitch a fancy button to the front just below the folded portion.

fold back upper edges

4 Slip the cozy over the wine bottle, adjusting the collar portion as needed. When serving the wine, remove the bottle from the cozy for easier pouring.

SewFast
Gift Ideas

HAND TOWEL ROLL-UP

*Hang this decorative towel holder on your
bathroom wall. It's the perfect place to hold
extra hand towels for your guests.*

44

Materials:

3 octagonal, unquilted placemats(18" x 13")
1 plastic curtain ring
1 small bouquet or wreath of dried flowers
fabric marker

Directions:

4½"- 5"

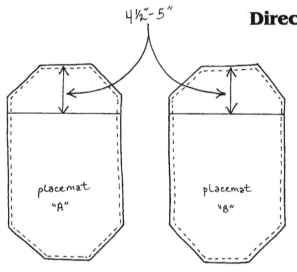

1 On the wrong sides of two of the place-mats (A and B), draw a line using a fabric marker across the short ends, 4 1/2" - 5" down from the edge.

2 With wrong sides together, fold the third placemat (C) in half matching the short ends. Pin the upper edges of C along the drawn line of placemat B. Stitch along the hemline of C to secure.

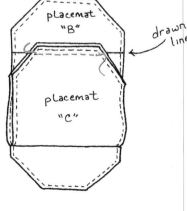

drawn line

3 With wrong sides together, fold B in half and pin to A along the drawn line as before. Stitch along the hemline of B to secure.

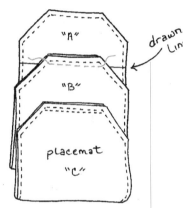

drawn line

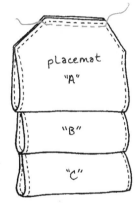

4 With wrong sides together, fold A in half and stitch the upper edges together along its hemline.

ring for hanging

5 On the back, upper edge of placemat A, whipstitch a ring to the center. Attach a small bouquet of dried flowers or a small embellished wreath to the front of the holder, centering over the ring. Roll your hand towels and place one in each section (A, B, and C) of the holder.
Note: Look for decorative dried-flower napkin rings to use at the top of the towel holder.

Chapter 4

BAGS GALORE

Any shape, any size and for any occasion, too! Stitch up a quick bag for your next sewing project.

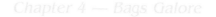

POCKET PORTFOLIO

*Carry important papers and books in this slim briefcase
complete with side pockets for smaller items.*

Materials:

2 rectangular placemats(17" x 12 1/2")
1 coordinating napkin
2 1/2 yds of webbing

Directions:

1 Cut the napkin in half. Fold and press each section in half again placing the hemmed edges opposite the folded edge.

2 Find the center point along the long edge of both mats. Center and pin a pressed napkin section along the lower edge of each placemat with the hemmed edge at the bottom and the folded edge at the top. Stitch across the bottom edge along the placemat hem.

3 Cut the webbing in half. Fold in 1/4" along each end of the webbing pieces. Beginning at the bottom edges, pin one piece of webbing over the side raw edges of the pocket forming the handle. Stitch in place. Repeat this procedure with the remaining piece of webbing and placemat.

fold under ¼"

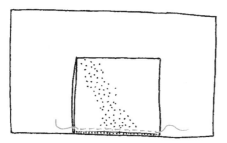

4 With wrong sides together, pin the placemats and stitch along the two short sides and across the lower edge. Use a triple straight stitch or a narrow zigzag for added strength.

FRINGED CARRY-ALL

Construct this sturdy bag with short handles or made-to-order shoulder straps. It's the ideal carry-all for almost anything.

Materials:

2 woven placemats, fringed on short ends(17" x 12")
3 yds of 1 1/2"-wide webbing
fabric marker

Directions:

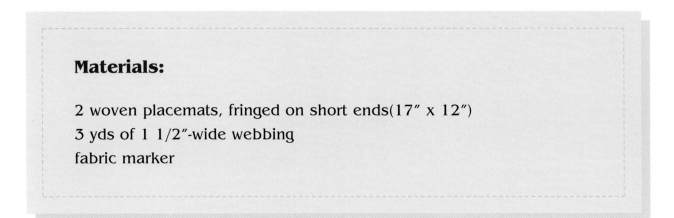

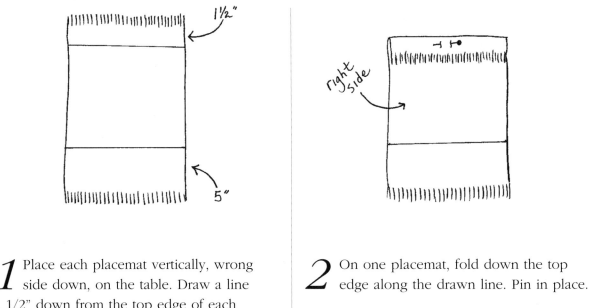

1 Place each placemat vertically, wrong side down, on the table. Draw a line 1 1/2" down from the top edge of each placemat. Draw another line 5" up from the bottom.

2 On one placemat, fold down the top edge along the drawn line. Pin in place.

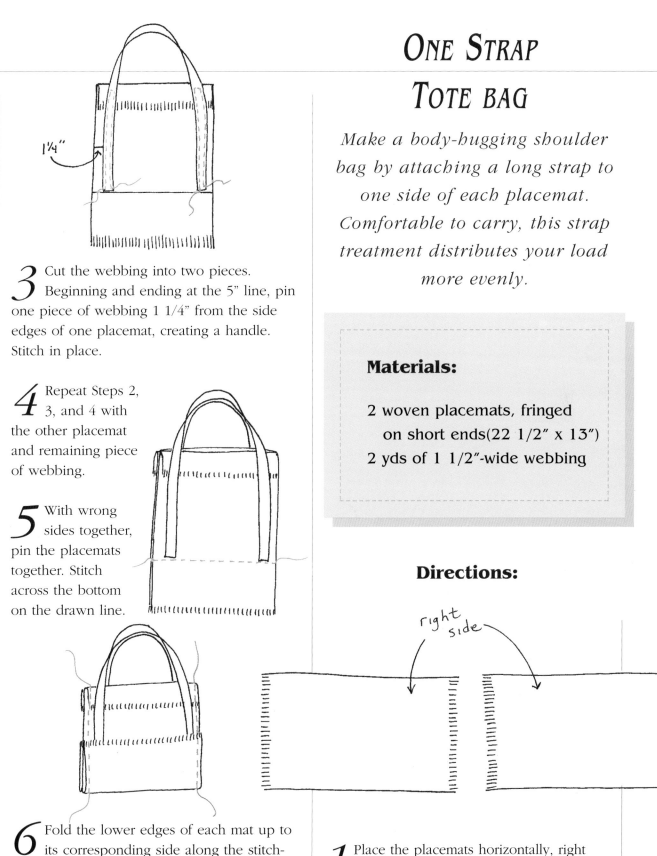

ONE STRAP TOTE BAG

Make a body-hugging shoulder bag by attaching a long strap to one side of each placemat. Comfortable to carry, this strap treatment distributes your load more evenly.

3 Cut the webbing into two pieces. Beginning and ending at the 5" line, pin one piece of webbing 1 1/4" from the side edges of one placemat, creating a handle. Stitch in place.

1¼"

4 Repeat Steps 2, 3, and 4 with the other placemat and remaining piece of webbing.

5 With wrong sides together, pin the placemats together. Stitch across the bottom on the drawn line.

6 Fold the lower edges of each mat up to its corresponding side along the stitching line. Sew each side of the bag from the bottom edge to the top through all layers.

Materials:

2 woven placemats, fringed on short ends(22 1/2" x 13")
2 yds of 1 1/2"-wide webbing

Directions:

right side

1 Place the placemats horizontally, right side up and side by side, on the table.

51

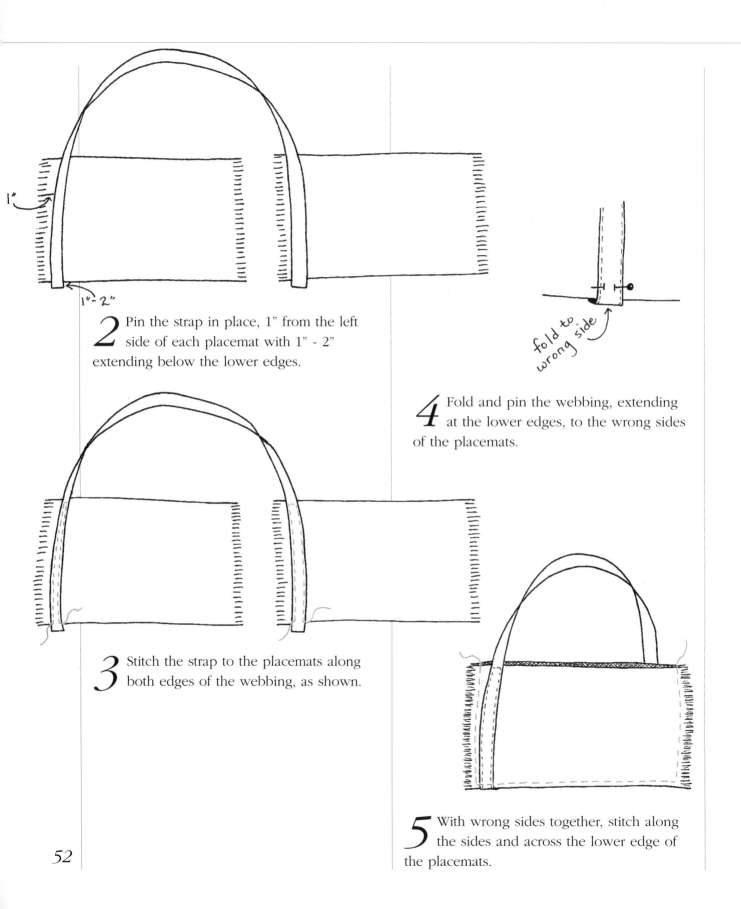

2 Pin the strap in place, 1" from the left
   side of each placemat with 1" - 2"
extending below the lower edges.

1"

1"- 2"

fold to wrong side

4 Fold and pin the webbing, extending
   at the lower edges, to the wrong sides
of the placemats.

3 Stitch the strap to the placemats along
   both edges of the webbing, as shown.

5 With wrong sides together, stitch along
   the sides and across the lower edge of
the placemats.

52

EASY BEACH TOTE

*Throw sunglasses, lotion, and your favorite book
into this shoulder bag and head for the beach!*

EASY BEACH TOTE

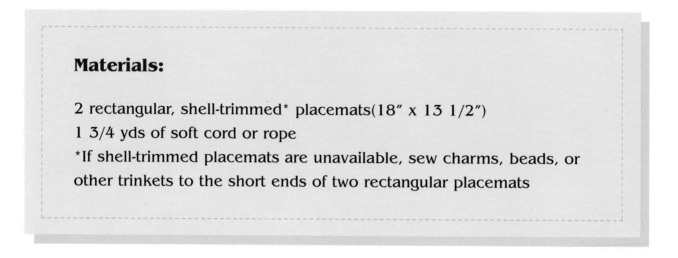

Materials:

2 rectangular, shell-trimmed* placemats(18" x 13 1/2")

1 3/4 yds of soft cord or rope

*If shell-trimmed placemats are unavailable, sew charms, beads, or other trinkets to the short ends of two rectangular placemats

Directions:

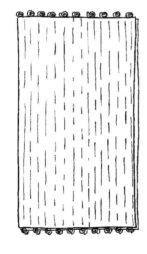

1 With wrong sides together, place the placemats vertically on the table.

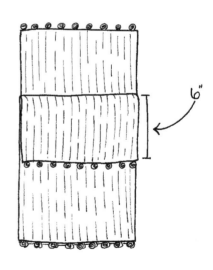

6"

2 Fold down the upper edge of the front placemat 6".

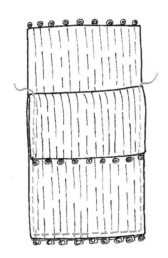

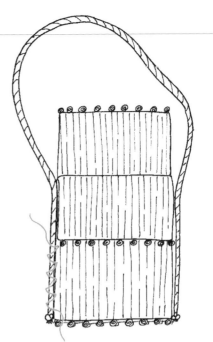

3 Stitch along each side from the folded edge to the bottom of the placemats. Stitch across the lower edge of the bag. **Note:** For reinforcement, use a triple straight stitch or a narrow zigzag stitch.

5 Zigzag the cord to the bag, setting the stitch width at a setting wide enough to stitch into the cord and also into the bag. Sew from each knot to the upper edge of the bag, being careful not to stitch into the flap. Hand-tack the knots to the lower side edges of the bag, if desired, to secure.

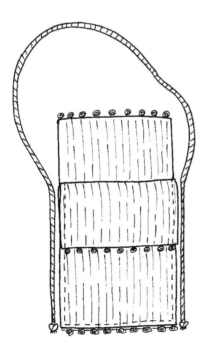

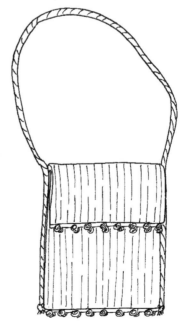

4 Tie a knot in each end of the cord. Place the ends of the cord on each side of the bag with the knots at the lower edge.

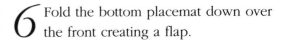

6 Fold the bottom placemat down over the front creating a flap.

Drawstring Bag

Change the look of a simple tote by adding a drawstring of decorative cording.

Materials:

2 cotton, woven placemats, fringed on short ends(20" x 13")
1 yd of decorative cording
1 3/4 yd of 1 1/4"-wide webbing
3/4 yd of 3/4"-wide elastic
18" of 1"-wide bias tape

Directions:

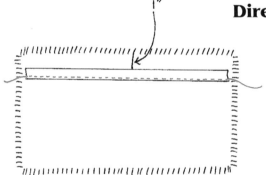

1 With right side down, pin the bias tape to the long side of one of the placemats, 1" from the edge. Edgestitch along one side of the bias tape, leaving the ends open.

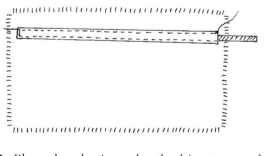

2 Place the elastic under the bias tape and stitch across one end, through the elastic. Using a zipper foot, stitch along the other edge of the bias tape without stitching into the elastic.

3 Pull the elastic from the unstitched end drawing the placemat up to about 10". Stitch across the end of the casing and trim any excess elastic.

56

4 Make six 3/4" buttonholes evenly spaced across one long side of the remaining placemat.

5 Cut the decorative cord into two pieces. Starting at the side edges and ending at the center of the placemat, thread each piece through 3 buttonholes. Pin or baste the end of the cord at the side edges.

wrong sides together

6 With wrong sides together, pin the two placemats with the elastic and the buttonholes at the top edge. Stitch across the lower edge, 1/4" - 1/2" from the edge, above the fringe.

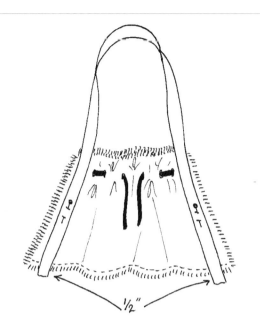

1"

1/2"

7 Fold back 1/2" at each end of the webbing piece. Beginning along one side, pin the webbing to the top mat and continuing down the other side, creating the handle.

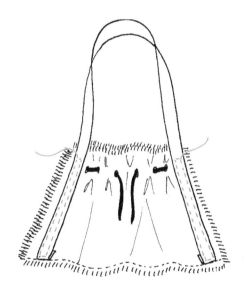

8 Stitch along each edge of the webbing through all layers, as shown, securing the decorative cord and the ends of the bias casing in the stitching. Use a zigzag stitch for additional strength, if desired. Tie the decorative cord together at the center front. Add trinkets or beads, or knot the ends of the cords.

SHAPED TOTE

This uniquely shaped tote has durable, padded handles made from real or imitation leather or suede.

Materials:

2 octagonal placemats(17″ x 12″)

2 strips of Ultrasuede® or leather(18″ x 4″)

4 - 2 1/4″ squares of Ultrasuede® or leather

32″ of 1″ cotton cording

3″ of 1/2″-wide Velcro™

Directions:

1 On the wrong side of one octagonal placemat, draw lines from corner to corner, as shown.

drawn lines

2 With right sides together, pin the placemats in place. Stitch together along the drawn lines and across the bottom edge. Turn the placemats to the right side and use a point turner to sharpen the corners.

3 To make each handle, center a piece of cord on the wrong side of the suede strip and wrap.

4 Using a zipper foot, stitch along the long edge, close to the cord.

Stitch, using a zipper foot

5 Trim the seam allowance as close to the stitching as possible.

trim close to stitching

6 Place the uncorded ends of the handles, 1 1/2″ from the upper corners of the bag and pin. The trimmed seams of the handles should be placed to the inside.

1½″

7 Fold each square of suede diagonally. Pin each triangular piece over the ends of the handles onto the bag. Edgestitch each piece to the bag, being sure to stitch through the ends of the handles.

59

Chapter 5

FOR KIDS ONLY

*Use these projects
as a simple
method to teach
your own children
to sew. They're
great as birthday
presents for that
special someone.*

ACTIVITY APRON

Use this fun apron to protect a child's clothing
when she paints, draws, or plays with clay.

Materials:

1 octagonal, brightly colored, vinyl placemat(17 1/2" x 12 1/2")
2 1/2 yds of 1/2"-wide grosgrain ribbon
4 brightly colored, large buttons
1 spring-lock closure (optional)

Directions:

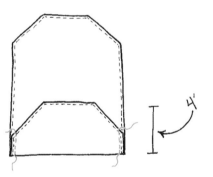

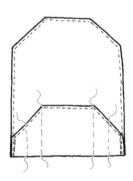

1 With wrong side down and the placemat placed vertically on the table, fold up the lower edge 4" to form the pocket. Straight-stitch along each side edge.

2 Stitch vertical lines through all layers from each corner of the newly formed pocket to the folded edge. Stitch additional vertical lines on each side equidistant between the side seams and the previous rows of stitching.

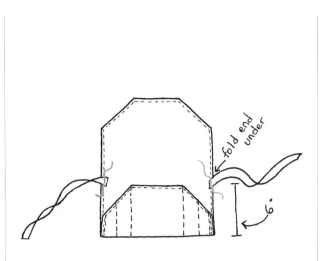

3 Cut the ribbon into 4 equal pieces. On one end of two pieces of ribbon, fold under 1/2". Stitch to each side edge, 6" up from the lower edge.

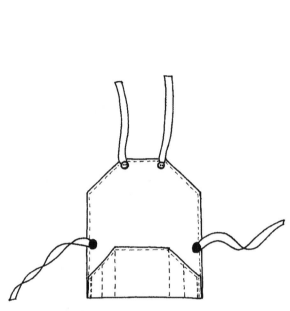

5 Stitch decorative buttons over the ends of the ribbon. Make a knot in the ends of the two side ties. Add a spring-lock closure to the neck ties.

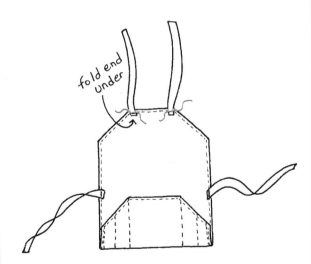

4 Fold under 1/2" on one end of the remaining two pieces of ribbon and stitch them to the placemat at the top corners.

LITTLE ARTIST CASE

The perfect place for any young artist's coloring books and drawing paper, this case also has a special pocket for crayons and markers.

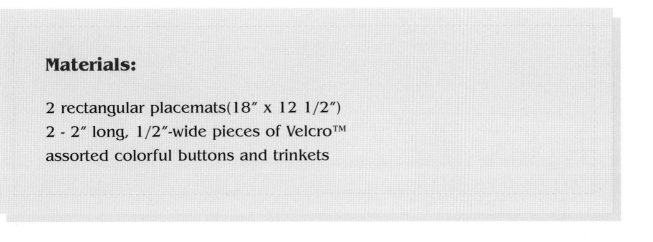

Materials:

2 rectangular placemats(18" x 12 1/2")
2 - 2" long, 1/2"-wide pieces of Velcro™
assorted colorful buttons and trinkets

Directions:

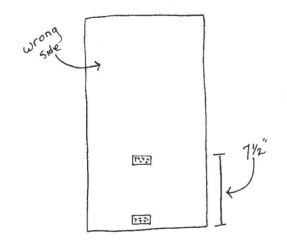

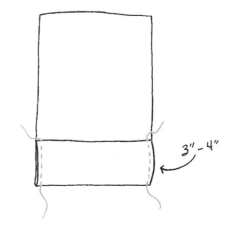

1 On the wrong side of one placemat, stitch the looped side of one piece of Velcro™ in the center of the lower edge. Center and stitch the hook side, 7 1/2" above the lower edge and the other Velcro™ piece.

2 Fold up the lower edge, securing the Velcro™ strips. Stitch along the side edges of the placemat to form a pocket that is 3" - 4" in depth.

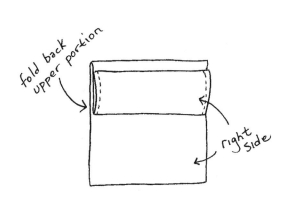

3 Fold the remaining section of the same placemat to the back, extending below the pocket as shown.

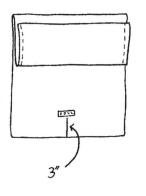

4 On the right side of the placemat, stitch the looped side of the remaining piece of Velcro™, 3" up from the lower edge.

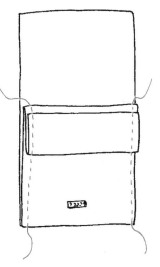

5 Place the folded placemat on the wrong side of the remaining placemat, matching the lower edges. Stitch along the side edges and at the bottom through all layers to form the pocket.

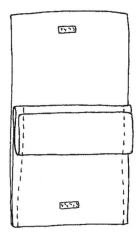

6 Centered on the wrong side of the upper edge of the flap, stitch the hook side of the Velcro™ piece to match the piece at the lower edge.

7 Close the flap over the pockets and sew assorted buttons to the outside to decorate the case.

BABY BIB

Make mealtime fun with this oversized,
vinyl bib with detachable pacifier.

Materials:

1 octagonal, brightly colored, vinyl placemat(17" x 11 1/2")
1 1/4 yds double-folded bias tape
2 plastic snaps
1 pacifier with ring handle

Directions:

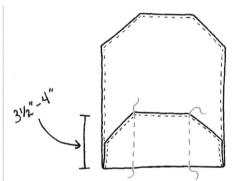

1 With wrong side down and the placemat placed vertically on the table, fold up the lower edge 3 1/2" - 4" to form a pocket. Stitch from each corner to the fold.

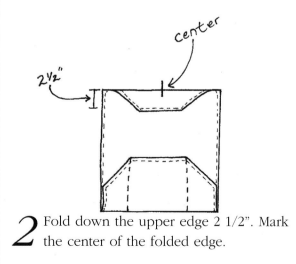

2 Fold down the upper edge 2 1/2". Mark the center of the folded edge.

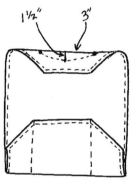

3 Measure and mark points 3" to each side of the center point and 1 1/2" down from the folded edge. Connect the

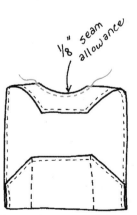
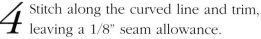

4 Stitch along the curved line and trim, leaving a 1/8" seam allowance.

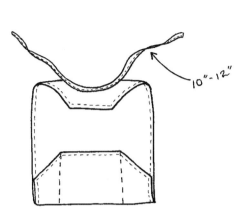

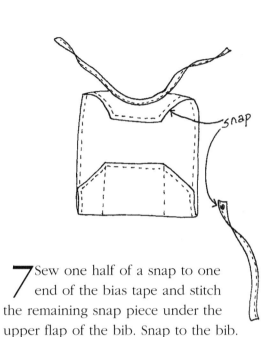

5 With 10" to 12" extending at each side of the neck curve, stitch the double-fold bias binding to the curved edge. Tie a knot in each end of the binding.

7 Sew one half of a snap to one end of the bias tape and stitch the remaining snap piece under the upper flap of the bib. Snap to the bib.

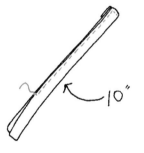

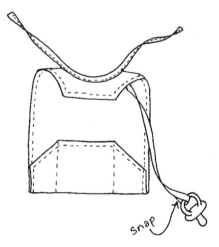

6 Cut a piece of double-folded bias binding 10" long. Fold each end under 1/4" and stitch. Stitch along the open edge to form a strap for the pacifier.

8 Sew one half of the second snap to the other end of the bias tape and stitch the remaining snap piece 1 1/2" from the end of the bias tape. Slip the end of the tape through the handle of the pacifier and snap.

DOLL CADDY

Here is a home for dolly and her wardrobe or that favorite stuffed animal family. Just fold up the handy carry-all and take her with you.

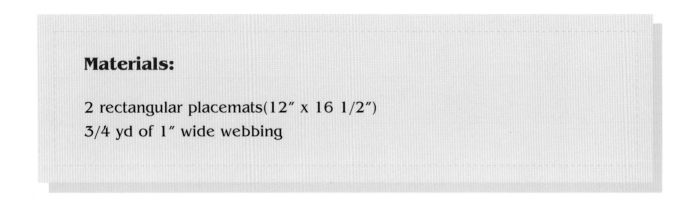

Materials:

2 rectangular placemats(12" x 16 1/2")
3/4 yd of 1" wide webbing

Directions:

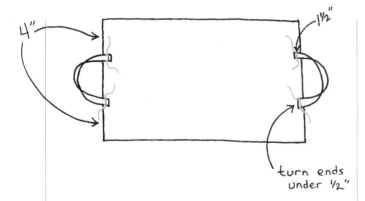

turn ends under 1/2"

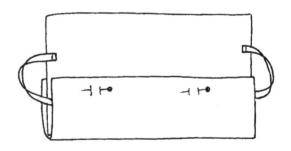

1 Cut the webbing into two equal pieces. Fold under 1/4" on each end of the webbing pieces and stitch each piece to the short edge of one placemat, as shown.

2 Fold the second placemat in half wrapping the lower edge of the first placemat, as shown. Pin in place.

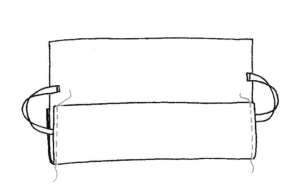

3 Stitch along the side edges through all layers to secure. The lower portion of each handle will be covered by the folded placemat.

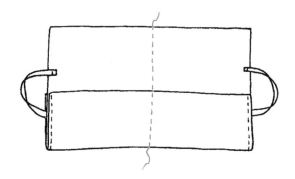

4 Fold the placemats in half, matching the handles. Mark the center points. Stitch along the center point to form the pockets.

5 Place the doll in the front pocket and use the other pockets for doll clothes.

HALLOWEEN TREAT BAG

This handy pumpkin fabric bag will certainly
hold a year's worth of trick-or-treating!

Materials:

2 Halloween-motif placemats, any shape(16" x 12 1/2")
1 1/4 yds of 1"-wide webbing

Directions:

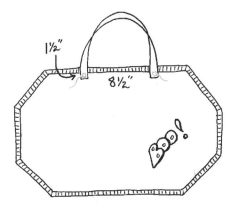

1 Cut the webbing into two equal pieces. Turn under the raw edges 1/2" and stitch each piece of webbing 1 1/2" from the top edge of each placemat, centered as shown.

2 With wrong sides together, pin the two placemats. Stitch along the hemline on the sides and across the bottom forming the bag. Now watch out for goblins!

Chapter 6

PRETTY PURSES

*Design any
number of handy,
quick purses for
yourself from
pretty placemats.*

TUXEDO EVENING BAG

*Tailored and elegant, this tucked bag with a hint
of glitter is perfect for a night on the town.*

Materials:

1 black tuxedo placemat(17 1/2" x 13")
1 3/4 yds of gold or silver decorative cord
3" of 1/2"-wide Velcro™
assortment of decorative buttons
monofilament thread
polyester bobbin thread to match placemat

Directions:

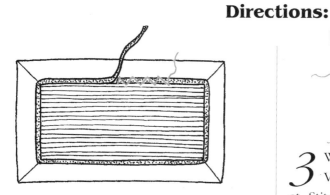

1 Using monofilament thread, couch the gold or silver cord along the inside of the border by zigzagging over the cord. Begin and end the stitching at the center, upper edge for inconspicuous results.

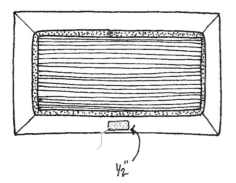

2 Center and stitch the hook side of the Velcro™ 1/2" from the lower edge, as shown.

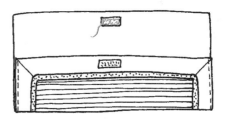

5½"

3 With wrong sides together, fold up the Velcro ™ end, 5 1/2" to form the pocket. Stitch along the sides to secure.

4 Stitch the loop section of Velcro™ to the wrong side of the flap in line with the hook section.

5 On the front of the flap, sew decorative buttons in a cluster over the Velcro™ stitching.

DEEP POCKET CLUTCH

*Plenty of pockets! This simple clutch purse has
one large outside and one large inside pocket.*

Materials:

1 octagonal, solid-colored placemat(17" x 12 1/2")
1 rectangular placemat in a coordinating print(18" x 12 1/2")
1 small, flat napkin ring for closure
10"-12" of 1/4"-wide ribbon

Directions:

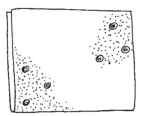

1 With wrong sides together, fold the printed placemat in half along the short side.

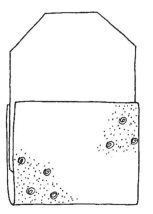

2 Position the octagonal placemat within the fold of the printed placemat, as shown.

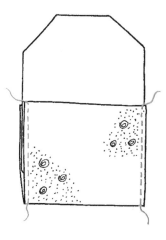

3 Stitch through all layers of the placemats, along both sides, following the hemline.

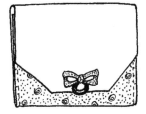

4 Tie a bow with the ribbon through the napkin ring. Centered near the lower edge, hand-stitch the bow and ring to the flap.

79

GOLD-TRIMMED SHOULDER BAG

This elegant shoulder bag uses a gold napkin ring to "weight" the flap and coordinate with the chain strap.

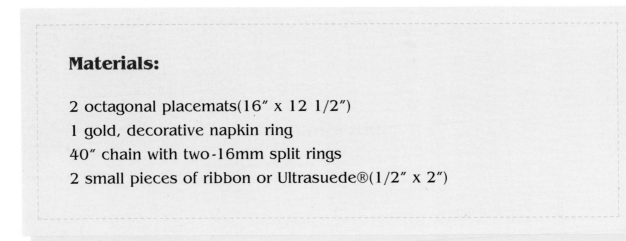

Materials:

2 octagonal placemats(16" x 12 1/2")
1 gold, decorative napkin ring
40" chain with two-16mm split rings
2 small pieces of ribbon or Ultrasuede®(1/2" x 2")

Directions:

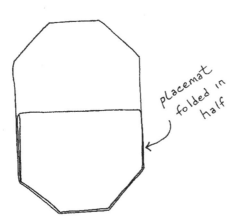

placemat folded in half

1 With wrong sides together, fold one placemat in half across the short side. With the fold to the center, place the folded placemat on the wrong side of the second placemat, matching the lower edges.

fold ribbon through ring

2 Fold each strip of ribbon or Ultrasuede® in half through a split ring, forming a loop.

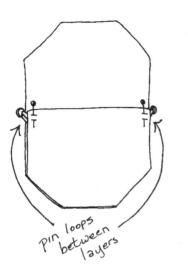

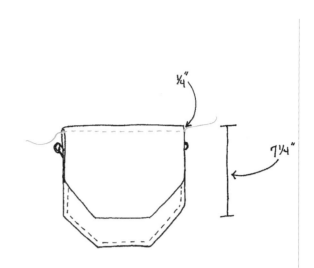

3 Pin each ring and loop between the folds along the upper edge of the folded placemat.

5 Fold the under placemat to the front creating a 7 1/4" flap. Stitch 1/4" from the folded edge.

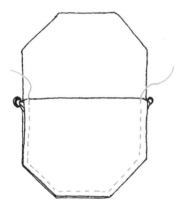

4 Stitch along the sides and the lower edge of the layered placemats, securing the rings and loops in the process.

6 Attach the chain strap to the jump rings. Bartack the decorative napkin ring to the front of the flap.

TAPESTRY POCKET

*Give this handy, shoulder-strap purse to a friend. This great
purse is large enough for the essentials, but small enough to wear
conveniently across your body.*

Materials:

1 rectangular, single layer, tapestry placemat, turned and stitched
   edges(18 1/2" x 12 1/2")
3/4 yd of 1 1/4"-wide ribbon or a strip of Ultrasuede® in a
   coordinating color
2 yds of 1/4"-diameter decorative cord
1" square of Velcro™
1 napkin ring or decorative closure
monofilament thread

Directions:

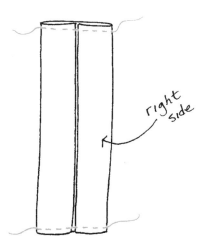

right side

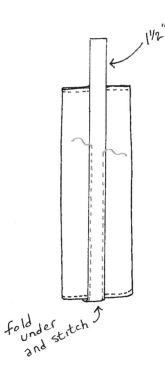

1½"

fold under and stitch

1 Position the placemat, vertically, right side down on the table. Fold the long hemmed edges in, meeting in the center. Edgestitch along the upper and lower edges, securing the layers together.

2 Pin the ribbon or Ultrasuede® piece down the center covering the edges of the placemat with 1 1/2" extending at each end. Edgestitch the trim in place, along both edges. Fold under the ends of the trim and edgestitch in place, matching the stitching with the previous line of stitching on the trim.

83

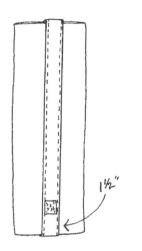

1½"

3 On the right side, position the hook side of the Velcro™ piece, 1 1/2" from the lower edge, centering it from side to side. Stitch in place.

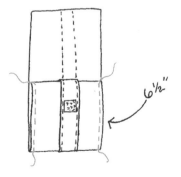

6½"

4 Turn the placemat placing the trimmed side down. Fold up the lower end 6 1/2" to form the pocket. Stitch along the side edges to secure.

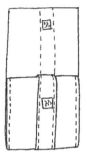

5 On the wrong side of the upper edge, stitch the loop section of Velcro™.

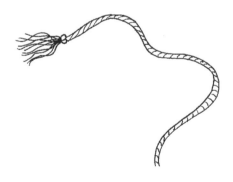

6 Tie a knot in one end of the decorative cord. If desired, tie the knot 3" - 4" from the end and fray the ends to create a tassel.

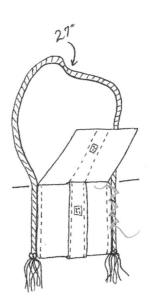

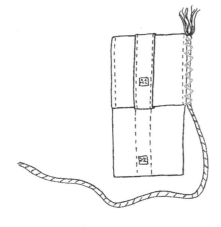

8 At the upper edge of the purse, reinforce the stitching. Leave about 27" of the cord free for the strap. Place the remaining cord along the right edge of the purse and couch as directed in step #7. After reinforcing the stitch, tie a knot in the cord and trim or fray to match the left side of the bag.

7 With the flap open and the purse positioned upside down, place the cord along the left edge of the purse. Using monofilament cord and a zigzag stitch, couch the cord along the edge of the purse, adjusting the width of the stitch to swing over the cord and into the air. As the needle swings back, it will stitch into the fabric of the purse.

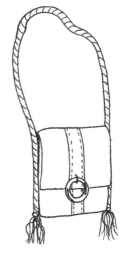

9 Bartack the napkin ring or decorative closure to the front flap.

FOLD-OVER CLUTCH

*This quick-to-make purse has three pockets
including a "secret" one in the flap.*

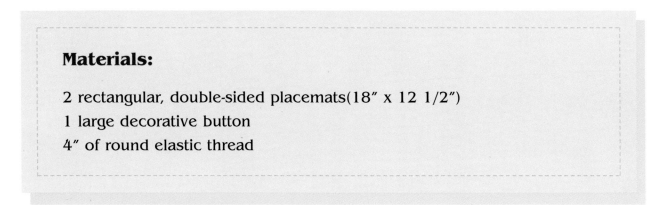

Materials:

2 rectangular, double-sided placemats(18" x 12 1/2")
1 large decorative button
4" of round elastic thread

Directions:

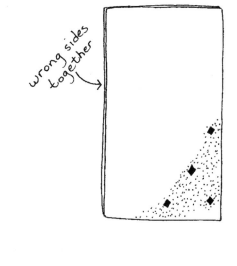

wrong sides together

1 With wrong sides together, place the
placemats on the table vertically.

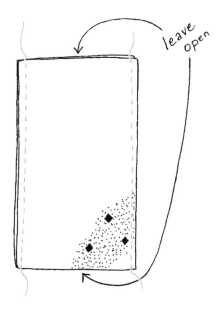

leave open

2 Stitch along the sides, leaving the upper
and the lower edges open.

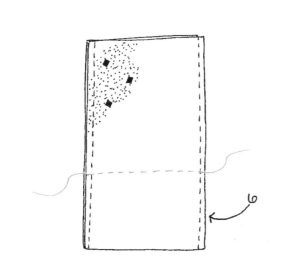

3 Make a mark 6 1/2" from the lower edge. Straight-stitch across the width of the placemat through both layers at the mark.

stitch inside through one layer only

5 Make a loop from the elastic thread. Bartack to the center of the flap, stitching through the outer layer only.

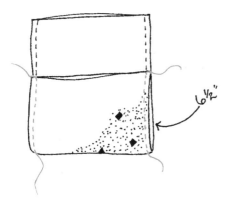

4 Fold up the lower edge along the stitched line to form the body of the purse. Stitch both side edges over the previous stitching line to secure.

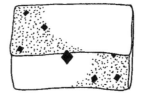

6 Fold the upper edge down creating the flap. Sew the decorative button to the front of the purse to match the elastic loop.

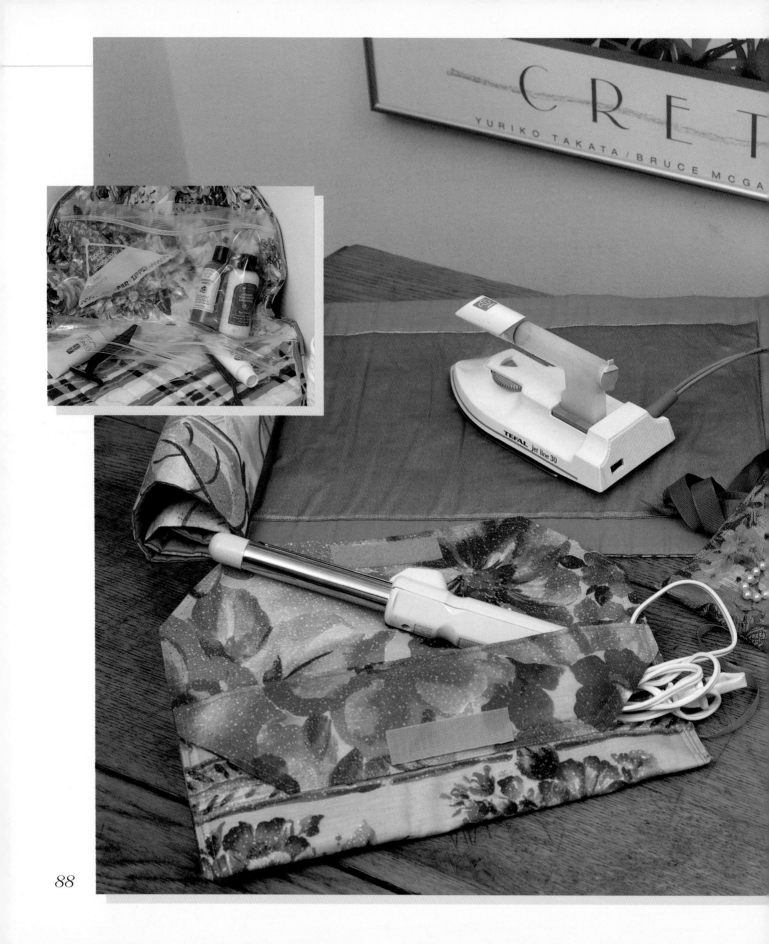

Chapter 7

TRAVEL TIME

Quick travel carry-alls make great gifts. They're easy to make, too!

CURLING IRON CADDY

*Pack your curling iron away while still warm in
this heat-resistant caddy with a separate cord corral which keeps
the cord from touching the hot barrel of the iron.*

Materials:

1 octagonal placemat(17" x 12 1/2")
1 piece of Teflon™ fabric, approximately 12" x 14"
3" of 1/2"-wide Velcro™

Directions:

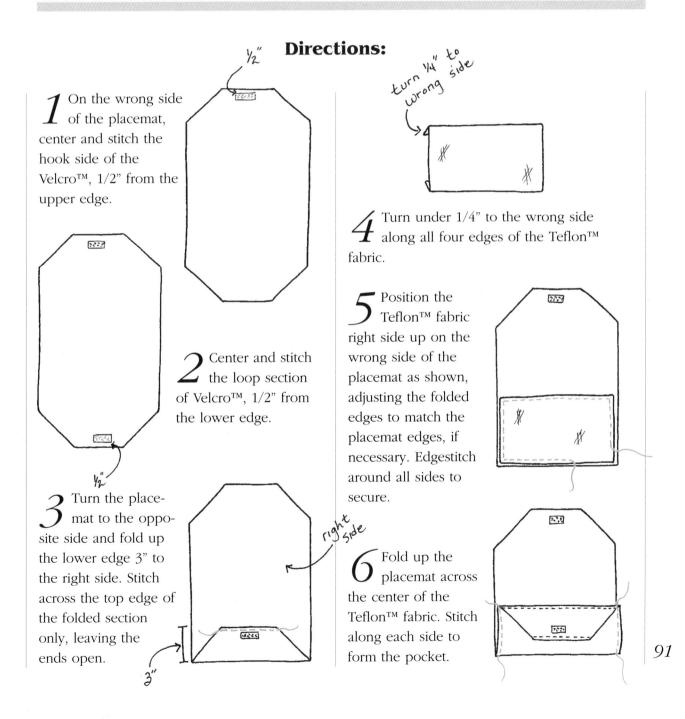

1 On the wrong side of the placemat, center and stitch the hook side of the Velcro™, 1/2" from the upper edge.

½"

2 Center and stitch the loop section of Velcro™, 1/2" from the lower edge.

½"

3 Turn the placemat to the opposite side and fold up the lower edge 3" to the right side. Stitch across the top edge of the folded section only, leaving the ends open.

3"

turn ¼" to wrong side

4 Turn under 1/4" to the wrong side along all four edges of the Teflon™ fabric.

5 Position the Teflon™ fabric right side up on the wrong side of the placemat as shown, adjusting the folded edges to match the placemat edges, if necessary. Edgestitch around all sides to secure.

right side

6 Fold up the placemat across the center of the Teflon™ fabric. Stitch along each side to form the pocket.

91

PORTABLE IRONING BOARD

Carry your own padded, heat-resistant ironing surface with you on your travels. Perfect for pressing on the go!

Materials:

2 rectangular, padded or quilted placemats(17" x 12")
33" x 10" piece of Teflon™-coated fabric
1/2 yd of 5/8"-wide ribbon

Directions:

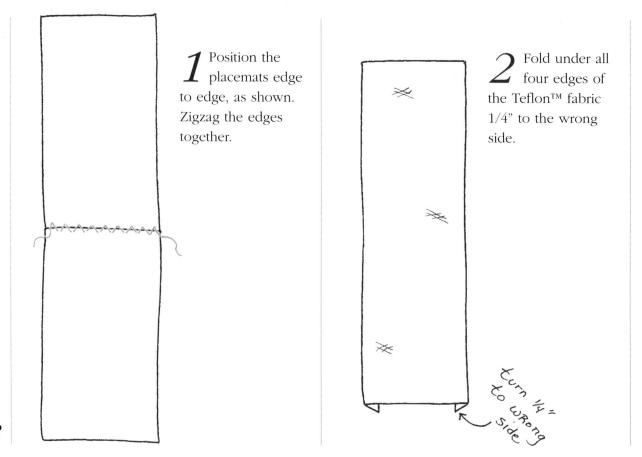

1 Position the placemats edge to edge, as shown. Zigzag the edges together.

2 Fold under all four edges of the Teflon™ fabric 1/4" to the wrong side.

turn 1/4" to wrong side

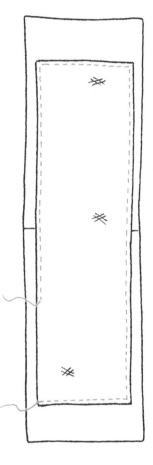

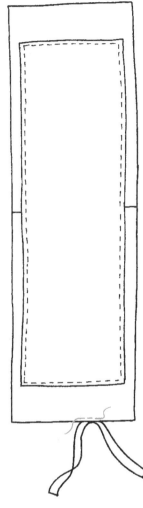

4 Find the center of the ribbon by folding in half. Bartack the folded edge of the ribbon to the center of one end of the ironing mat along the outside edge.

3 Pin the Teflon™ fabric to the wrong side of the sewn placemats, centering it as shown. Edgestitch the Teflon™ fabric in place around all edges.

5 When traveling, roll the ironing mat tightly, starting at the end without the ribbon. Wrap and tie the ribbon around it to hold.

MINI JEWELRY CASE

This four-pocket, fold-up jewelry case protects your valuables in a small compact package, making it easy to pack in your suitcase or handbag.

Materials:

1 rectangular, double- or single-sided placemat(16 1/2" x 13")
5/8 yd of 3/8"-wide ribbon
4" of 3/4"-wide Velcro™
fabric marker
3" square of plastic canvas (optional)

Directions:

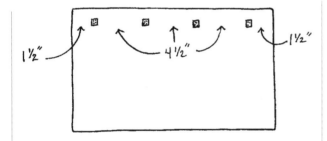

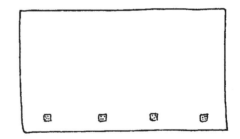

1 Cut the Velcro™ strip into 4 equal pieces. On the right side of the placemat, stitch the hook half of each piece along one long edge, spaced as shown

2 On the wrong side of the placemat, stitch the loop half of each piece of Velcro™ along the opposite edge, spacing them to correspond with the first pieces.

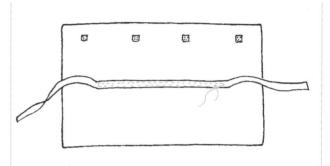

4 Center the ribbon over the drawn line. The ends of the ribbon will extend beyond the edges of the placemat. Stitch the ribbon to the placemat between the marked points on the drawn line.

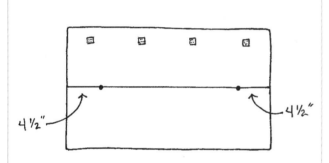

4 ½"   4 ½"

3 On the right side, draw a horizontal line across the center of the placemat. Measure 4 1/2" from each end and mark on the drawn line.

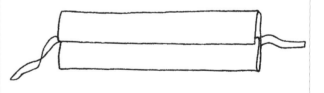

5 Fold the top edge of the placemat down and the lower edge up, matching the Velcro™ pieces.

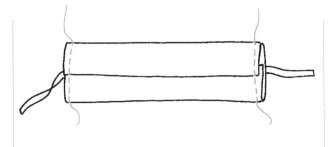

6 Stitch along the side hemlines of the placemat to secure the edges. Be careful not to stitch the ends of the ribbon in the seams.

8 Place your jewelry in each pocket. Place earrings on plastic canvas (optional). Fold each end to the center and then fold to the center again. Tie the ribbon ends together to hold the roll in place.

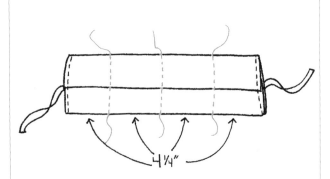

4 ¼"

7 Again leaving the ribbon ends free, stitch a vertical line down the center through all layers. Stitch two additional lines, 4 1/2" on either side of the center, creating 4 equal pockets.

TRAVEL TOILETRY BAG

*This functional, folded travel bag has waterproof
pockets and a zippered section for personal items.*

Materials:

2 octagonal, quilted placemats(18" x 13")
1- 14" zipper
3 - 5 zippered plastic bags in assorted sizes
14" of 1" single-folded bias tape
3" of 1/2"-wide Velcro™

Directions:

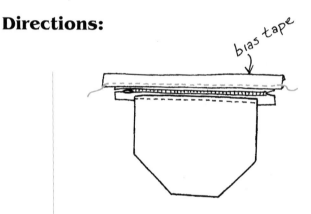

fold under 1/4"

bias tape

1 Select one placemat for the inside of the bag. Cut it in half across the width. Fold under 1/4" along the cut edge and top-stitch to one side of the zipper tape, next to the coils.

2 Place the folded bias tape along the other side of the zipper tape and stitch next to the coils.

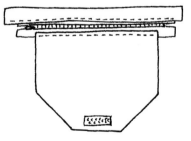

3 On the right side, position the hook side of the Velcro™ piece, 1 1/2" from the lower edge, centering it from side to side. Stitch in place.

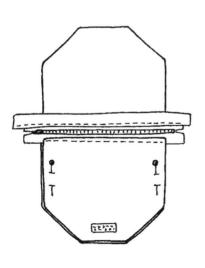

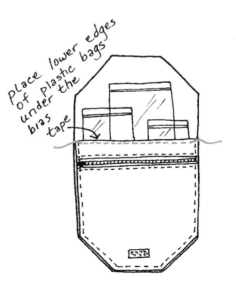

Place lower edges of plastic bags under the bias tape

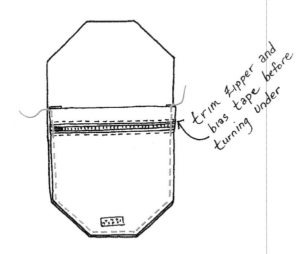

trim zipper and bias tape before turning under

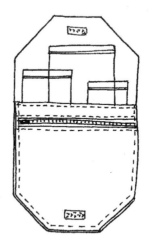

4 With wrong sides together and the outer edges even, place the zippered half on top of the outer placemat. Pin or baste in place.

5 Stitch the placemats together along the outer edges, folding in the ends of the zipper tape and bias tape on each side. **Note:** If the zipper is longer than the edge to which it is being stitched, unzip it before turning under the ends and stitching.

6 Place the lower edges of the plastic bags under the bias tape and pin. Edgestitch the bias tape to the placemat, catching the plastic bags at the same time.

7 On the wrong side of the outer place-mat, stitch the hook section of the Velcro™ piece in place, matching the position of the first.

SewFast
Gift Ideas
™

Chapter 8

STITCH
IN TIME

*Easy storage
compartments
make these
organizers the
perfect place to
keep all your
sewing and craft
essentials.*

SewFast
Gift Ideas

KNITTING NEEDLE ORGANIZER

Organize and store your knitting needles in this useful folder,
which also includes a special pocket for circular needles.

Materials:

2 rectangular placemats(17" x 13")
13" of 3/4"-wide elastic
1 yd of 1 1/4"-wide grosgrain ribbon
1" of 3/4"-wide Velcro™

Directions:

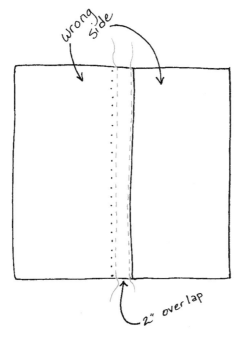

1 With wrong sides facing up, overlap the two placemats 2" along one long side. Stitch following the hemline of each placemat to secure.

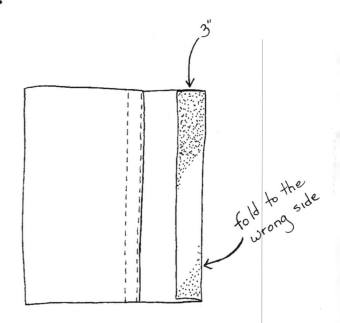

2 Fold back 3" to the wrong side along the right edge of the overlapped placemats.

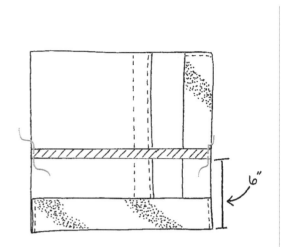

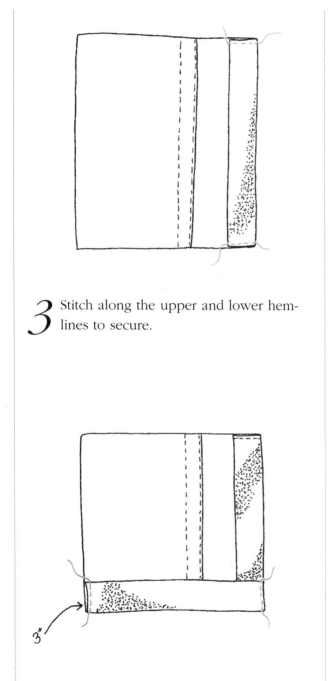

3 Stitch along the upper and lower hem-lines to secure.

5 Pin the elastic in place across the place-mats, 6" up from the lower edge. Stitch across the ends of the elastic to secure.

4 Along the lower edge, fold up 3" to the wrong side. Stitch along the side edges to secure.

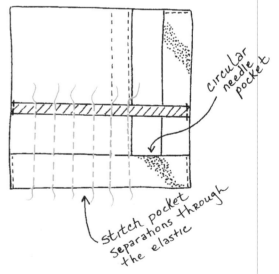

circular needle pocket

Stitch pocket separations through the elastic

6 Beginning at the left edge of the folder, stitch vertical lines from the lower fold-ed edge to the top edge of the elastic, creating 6 small pockets.

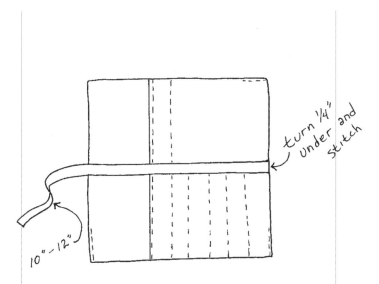

turn ¼"
under and
stitch

10" – 12"

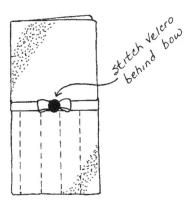

Stitch velcro
behind bow

7 On the right side of the folder, begin at the right edge and pin the ribbon above the elastic and vertical stitching lines. Turn the right end under about 1/4" and edgestitch the ribbon in place. The ribbon should extend 10" - 12" beyond the left edge of the folder.

9 Stitch a button in the center of the bow. Stitch the hook side of the Velcro™ behind the button. Fold the needle holder in half and wrap the ribbon around it. Stitch the loop section of the Velcro™ to the front of the folder at the appropriate point.

8 Fold the loose end of the ribbon back, as shown.

KNITTING BAG

Keep the yarn organized andready-to-go in this
handy bag supported by wooden dowels.

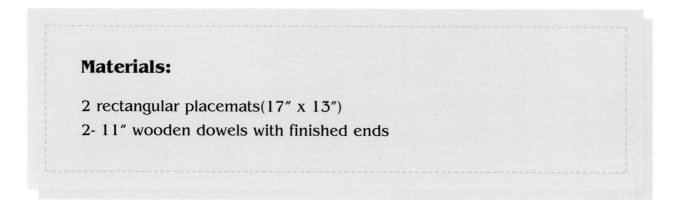

Materials:

2 rectangular placemats(17" x 13")
2- 11" wooden dowels with finished ends

Directions:

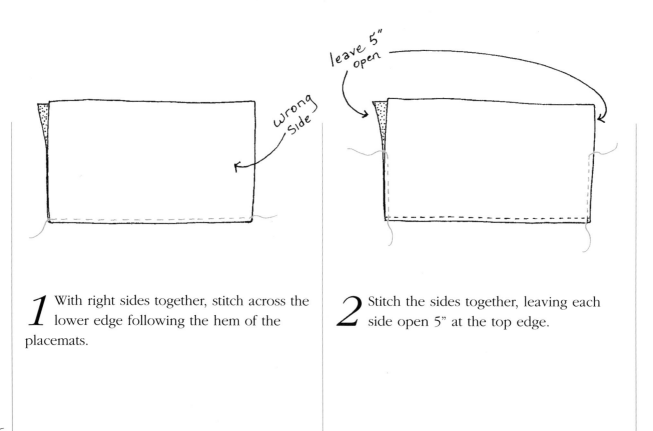

1 With right sides together, stitch across the lower edge following the hem of the placemats.

2 Stitch the sides together, leaving each side open 5" at the top edge.

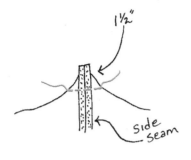

3 Along the bottom, fold the corners into a point, centering the seam. Stitch across the end, 1 1/2" down from the point.

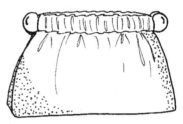

5 Slip the wooden dowels into the casings on each side. Place cardboard or plastic canvas, cut to fit, in the bottom of the bag for added support, if desired.

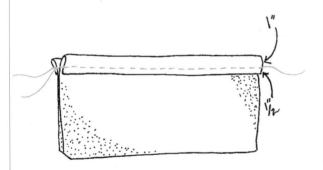

4 Turn the bag to the right side. Fold down each top edge, 1 1/2" to the outside. Stitch 1" from the folded top edges, following the hemline.

SewFast
Gift Ideas

PROJECT ORGANIZER

*Use this three-pocket folder for cross-stitch projects or
to take sewing supplies to classes. Great for
holding everything while traveling in the car.*

Materials:

3 rectangular placemats(16 1/2" x 13")
double-fold bias tape (optional)
toggle-type closure

Directions:

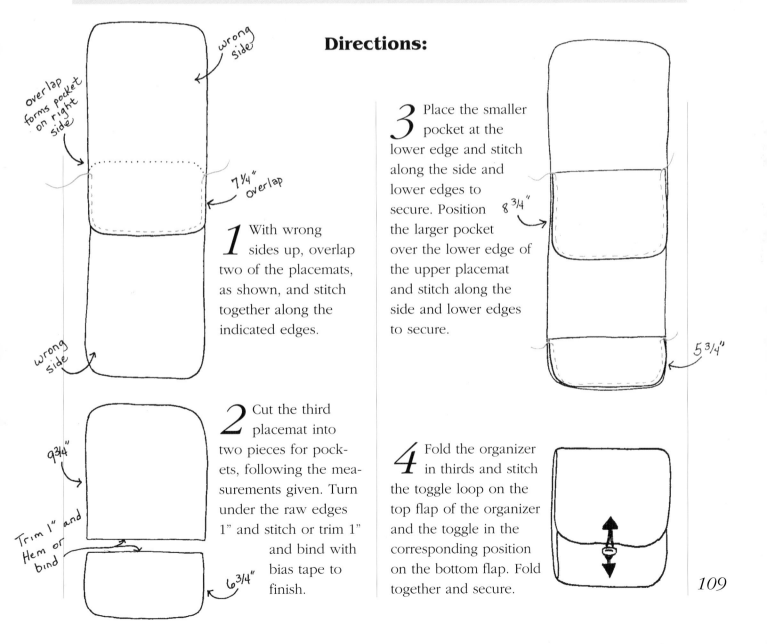

overlap forms pocket on right side

wrong side

7¼" overlap

1 With wrong sides up, overlap two of the placemats, as shown, and stitch together along the indicated edges.

wrong side

9¾"

Trim 1" and Hem or bind

6¾"

2 Cut the third placemat into two pieces for pockets, following the measurements given. Turn under the raw edges 1" and stitch or trim 1" and bind with bias tape to finish.

3 Place the smaller pocket at the lower edge and stitch along the side and lower edges to secure. Position the larger pocket over the lower edge of the upper placemat and stitch along the side and lower edges to secure.

8 ¾"

5 ¾"

4 Fold the organizer in thirds and stitch the toggle loop on the top flap of the organizer and the toggle in the corresponding position on the bottom flap. Fold together and secure.

CROCHET HOOK FOLDER

A quick way to organize crochet hooks
from the smallest to the largest.

Materials:

1 rectangular placemat(17" x 12")
3/4 yd of crocheted or "crochet-look" trim
2-10" pieces of 1/2"-wide ribbon

Directions:

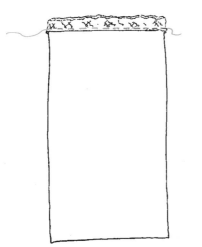

1 Pin the trim across one short end of the
placemat, wrapping it around to cover
the front and the back. Stitch through all layers to secure.

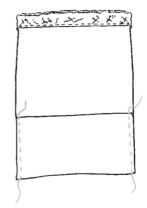

2 Fold up the opposite end 5" to the
wrong side. Stitch along the side edges
to make the pocket.

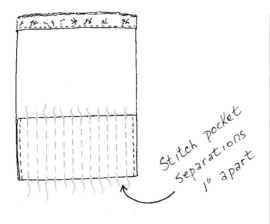

Stitch pocket separations 1" apart

3 Starting at the left side of the pocket, stitch vertical lines 1" apart until 12 pockets are made. The pockets can be made wider to accommodate larger hooks, if desired.

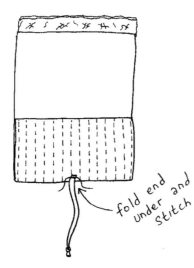

fold end under and stitch

4 Stitch one piece of ribbon to the lower center edge, turning under the end 1/4" to finish. Tie a knot in the unstitched end.

5 Stitch the other piece of ribbon in the center of the lace-trimmed edge, slipping the end under the lace. Tie the two ribbons together in a bow to close the folder.

MENDING CHATELAINE

*The ideal gift for your sewing buddy. All the tools
necessary for hand-sewing are located in one convenient place.*

Materials:

1 rectangular, quilted placemat(17" x 12")
1 yd of 3/4"-wide grosgrain ribbon
small amount of stuffing for pincushion

Directions:

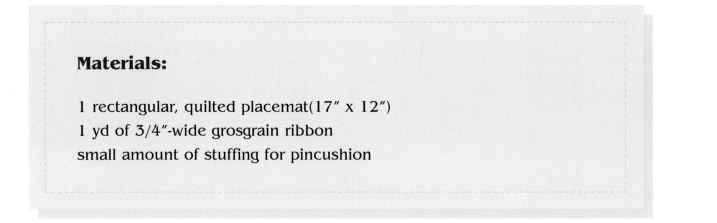

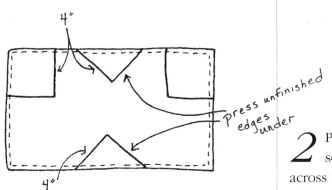

1 Cut two 4" squares from the placemat
corners, as shown. Cut 2 small triangles
from the side edges. Press the unfinished
edges of the triangles under a scant 1/4".

2 Position the triangles on top of the
squares with the finished edge going
across the middle of the square. The folded
edges of the triangles should fit along the finished edges of the squares. Stitch along these
edges to secure the pieces together.

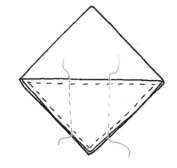

3 Stitch one or
two vertical
lines to create
small pockets.

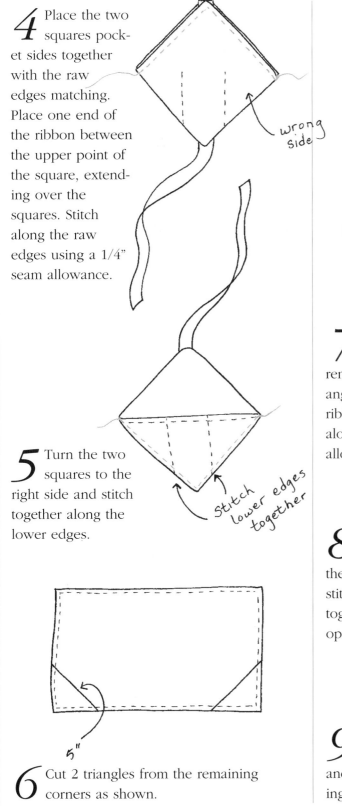

4 Place the two squares pocket sides together with the raw edges matching. Place one end of the ribbon between the upper point of the square, extending over the squares. Stitch along the raw edges using a 1/4" seam allowance.

wrong side

5 Turn the two squares to the right side and stitch together along the lower edges.

Stitch lower edges together

6 Cut 2 triangles from the remaining corners as shown.

5"

7 Place the triangles right sides together with the raw edges matching. Place the remaining end of the ribbon between the triangles at the center of the raw edge with the ribbon extending over the triangles. Stitch along the raw edges using a 1/4" seam allowance.

8 Turn the triangles to the right side and stitch the lower edges together, leaving a small opening for stuffing.

leave opening for stuffing

9 Stuff the pincushion and sew the opening closed.

113

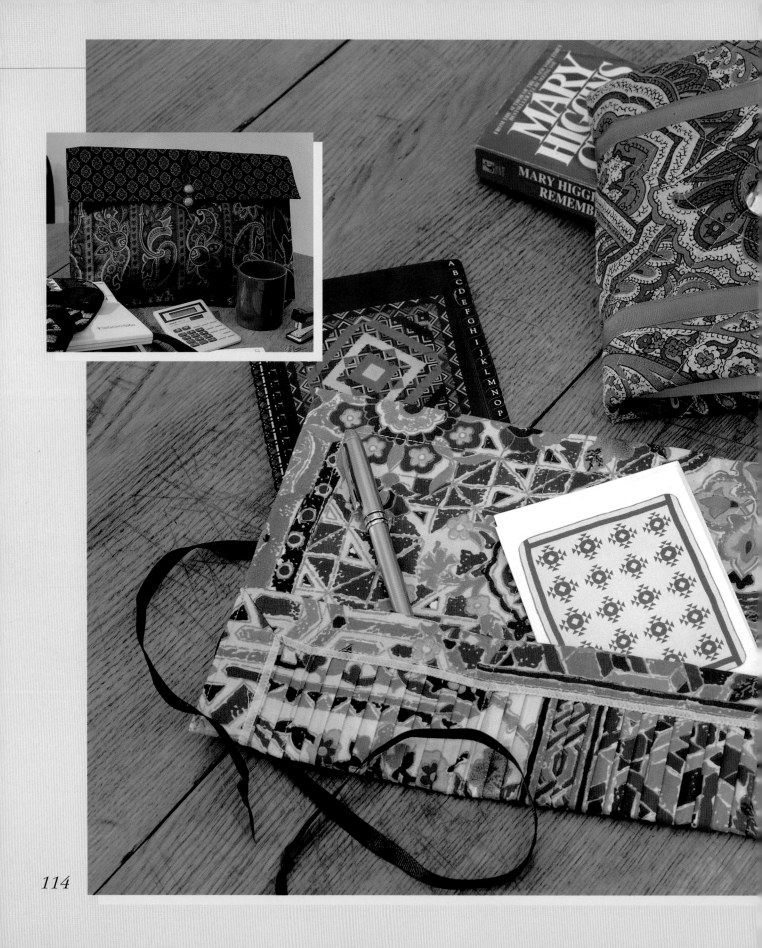

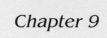

Chapter 9

HOME OFFICE

*Working at home
is the thing of
today! Accessorize
your office or help
a friend with these
handy placemat
ideas.*

BOOK BAG

This sturdy tote is perfect for taking books to and from the library. Or carry your laptop computer to your next job or on the plane.

Materials:

2 rectangular placemats, rounded corners(17 1/2" x 12 1/2")
2 yds of 2"-wide webbing in a coordinating color

Directions:

1 Cut two 25" pieces from the webbing. Turn under the short ends 1/4" and stitch the handles to each placemat near the upper edge as shown in the diagram. Stitch again about 1/4" from the first row of stitching to reinforce. Use a triple straight stitch or a zigzag stitch, if desired, for strength.

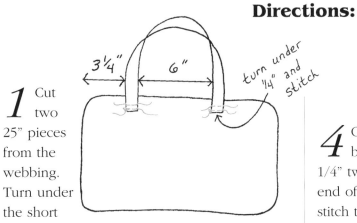

2 Starting 4" from the second row of stitching, fold the webbing together and edgestitch to make a more comfortable handle.

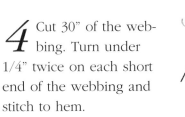

3 Mark 3" down from the top edges along the sides on the placemats.

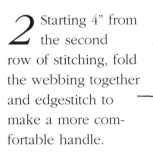

4 Cut 30" of the webbing. Turn under 1/4" twice on each short end of the webbing and stitch to hem.

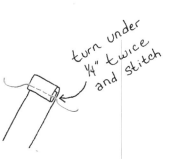

5 Starting at the marking, pin the webbing and one placemat wrong sides together, matching the edges. Stitch the two pieces together, down the side, across the lower edge, and up the opposite side. Repeat this procedure using the second placemat, attaching it to the opposite side of the book bag.

ENVELOPE PORTFOLIO

Use this classic portfolio as a briefcase for folders,
documents, and other important papers.

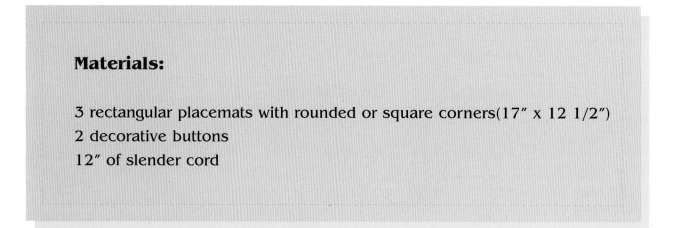

Materials:

3 rectangular placemats with rounded or square corners(17" x 12 1/2")
2 decorative buttons
12" of slender cord

Directions:

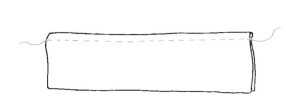

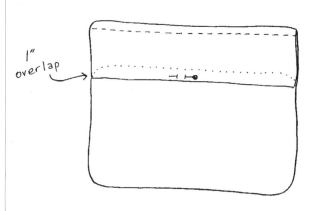

1 Fold one placemat in half across the width. Topstitch 1/4" from the folded edge creating the flap.

2 Overlap the open edges of the flap 1" along the long edge of one placemat, making the back of the portfolio. Pin in place.

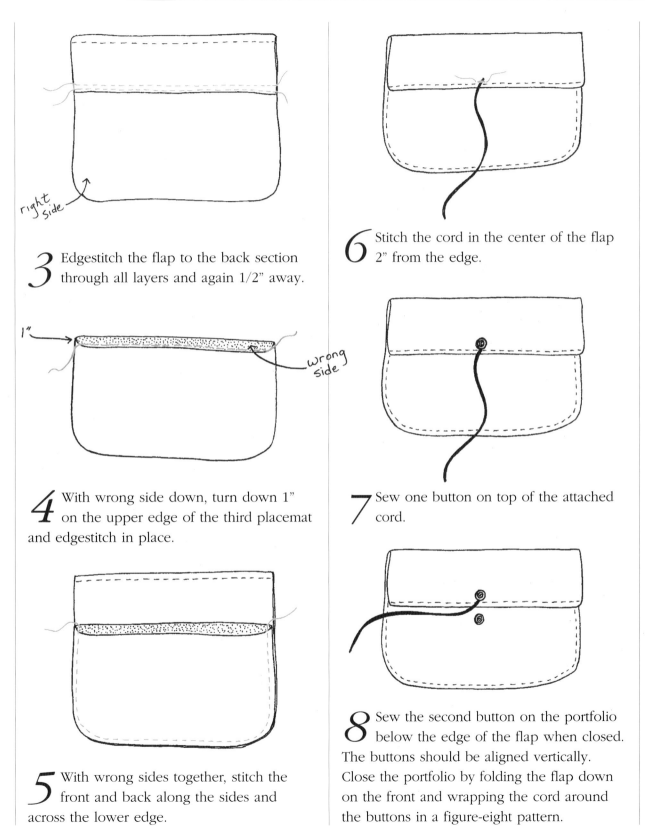

3 Edgestitch the flap to the back section through all layers and again 1/2" away.

4 With wrong side down, turn down 1" on the upper edge of the third placemat and edgestitch in place.

5 With wrong sides together, stitch the front and back along the sides and across the lower edge.

6 Stitch the cord in the center of the flap 2" from the edge.

7 Sew one button on top of the attached cord.

8 Sew the second button on the portfolio below the edge of the flap when closed. The buttons should be aligned vertically. Close the portfolio by folding the flap down on the front and wrapping the cord around the buttons in a figure-eight pattern.

119

STATIONERY FOLDER

*Keep note cards, envelopes, pen, and
stamps together in one place, ready for jotting
a few lines to a friend.*

Materials:

1 rectangular, double-sided placemat(17 1/2" x 12")
1 yd of 1/4"-wide grosgrain ribbon

Directions:

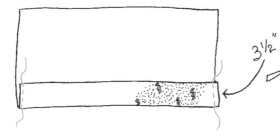

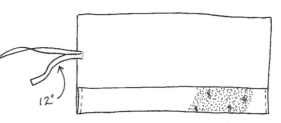

1 With wrong side up, fold up the lower edge 3 1/2" on one long side of the placemat. Stitch using the hemlines as a guide forming a pocket.

3 Fold back 12" on one end of the ribbon. Bartack the folded edge of the ribbon to the center of the left edge of the open folder.

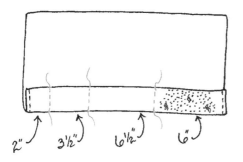

2 Straight-stitch vertical lines in the pocket, as shown, creating four sections for cards, envelopes, pen, and stamps.

4 Fold the placemat in thirds, starting on the right side and then the left. Wrap the longer end of the ribbon around the folder to the front and tie.

121

PAPERBACK BOOK COVER

Protect the privacy of your reading material with this quilted book cover. The nifty handles make it easy to carry anywhere.

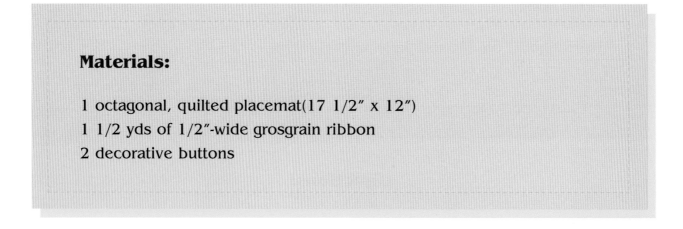

Materials:

1 octagonal, quilted placemat (17 1/2" x 12")
1 1/2 yds of 1/2"-wide grosgrain ribbon
2 decorative buttons

Directions:

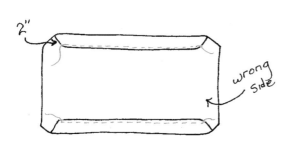

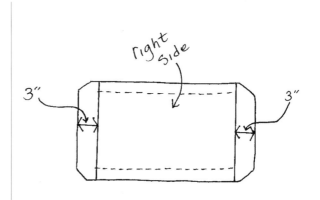

1 Fold under the long sides of the placemat 2" to the wrong side. Stitch to secure.

2 Measure in 3" from each short end and draw vertical lines on the right side of the placemat.

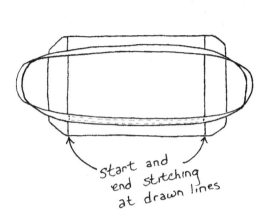

Start and
end stitching
at drawn lines

3 Cut 42" of the ribbon. Overlap and stitch the ends together to form a loop. Pin in place on the book cover over the previous lines of stitching. Edgestitch the ribbon in place, starting and ending on the drawn lines, as shown.

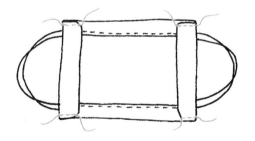

4 Fold the end flaps, to the wrong side, along the drawn lines. Stitch along the upper and lower edges to secure.

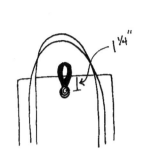

1 ¼"

5 Fold 8" of the ribbon into a loop and stitch it to the center of one of the shorter edges, 1 1/4" from the edge. Sew a decorative button on top of the raw edges.

6 Sew the second button on the opposite edge of the book cover in the appropriate place. To close the cover, slip the loop over this button.

INDEX

SUSAN BECK

has a degree in Textiles and Clothing and Master's Degree in Design. Her long association with Bernina of America as a District Sales Manager, Educator, and Education Editor has kept her informed about the latest and the best machines, tools, and techniques in the sewing industry. Susan has co-authored two books, "Elegant Beading for Your Sewing Machine and Serger" published by Sewing Information Resources/Sterling and "Fabric Crafts & Other Fun with kids" published by Chilton. Her first book, "Second Stitches: Recycle as You Sew" was published in 1993 and has been selected by Book of the Month Club many times.